AF328762

LET THEM SEE YOU

LET THEM SEE YOU

EMPOWERING **CHANGE** THROUGH **AUTHENTICITY**

MADISON BUTLER

WILEY

Library of Congress Cataloging-in-Publication Data is Available:

Names: Butler, Madison author
Title: Let them see you : empowering change through authenticity / Madison
  Butler.
Description: Hoboken, New Jersey : Wiley, [2026] | Includes index.
Identifiers: LCCN 2025023958 (print) | LCCN 2025023959 (ebook) | ISBN
  9781394294305 cloth | ISBN 9781394294312 adobe pdf | ISBN 9781394294329
  epub
Subjects: LCSH: Psychology, Industrial | Diversity in the workplace |
  Authenticity (Philosophy)
Classification: LCC HF5548.8 .B88 2026 (print) | LCC HF5548.8 (ebook)
LC record available at https://lccn.loc.gov/2025023958
LC ebook record available at https://lccn.loc.gov/2025023959

Cover Design: Paul McCarthy
Cover Art: © Getty Images | Colors Hunter–Chasseur De Couleurs
Printed and bound by CPI Group (UK) Ltd, Croydon, CR0 4YY
C9781394294305_270825

Contents

You Are Worthy of Being You

This isn't a business book. It's not a self-help book either. This is a *you* book.

You deserve to take up space. To breathe deeply. To move through the world as yourself—not as some polished, filtered, socially acceptable version of you, but *you*. In all your brilliance, all your flaws, your mess, your shame, all your contradictions, all your humanity.

You are not broken. You are not behind. You are not something that needs fixing.

You are a *work in progress*, and that is a beautiful thing.

The world around you will try to convince you that you are not good enough. It will try to tell you need to be more this, less that. That you need to shrink to fit into a box someone else made for you. The world will tell you that you must lean toward their idea of professionalism and beauty and anything less is unacceptable.

They want you to think that you need to package yourself into something more digestible, more marketable, more acceptable, more palpable.

So, they can sell you another cream, another fad diet, another fashion trend, another miracle medication.

Your body, your skin, your hair, your voice, your laugh, your stretch marks, your dimples, your quirks, your emotions, your dreams, your rage, your softness, your messiness—it all belongs because it is what makes you, you.

Your strengths and your struggles. Your joy and your rage. Your trauma and your healing. Your wins and your losses. Your love and your heartbreak. All of it matters, all of it deserves to exist out in the open.

You don't have to be perfect because perfect is a myth. You don't have to have it all figured out because no has it all figured it out. We are all winging it in one way or another.

You are already enough. Just as you are. Right now, in this moment, in this breath, you are enough.

And if no one has told you that lately, let me be the one to say it: *You are worthy of being you.*

Holistic and Human

This book isn't going to give you a checklist for how to fix your life. It won't tell you to follow five simple steps to success or map out a formula for happiness. It won't tell you how to snatch your waist or make your refrigerator Instragrammable.

Instead, this book is an exploration of self, of identity, of belonging. It's a conversation about what it means to be human in a world that so often asks us to be anything *but.*

It explores how we as humans can use our own humanity to show up for up for others to be better friends, better leaders, and better co-workers.

It's about unlearning the harmful narratives we've been fed. It's about reclaiming the parts of ourselves we were told to abandon. It's about stepping into our own power—not because we've finally *earned* it but because it was always ours to begin with.

Through these pages, we'll unpack ideas like:

- Knowing, deep in your bones, that you are already enough
- Accepting that being a work in progress is not a flaw but the journey of life
- Letting go of the pressure to be perfect
- Understanding that healing isn't about erasing the past; it's about learning to embrace it
- Questioning the structures that we have become complacent in
- Breaking cycles of harm, both for ourselves and for those who will follow in our footsteps
- Leading with authenticity, vulnerability, and humanity
- Making space for others while allowing ourselves to take space as well
- Calling out bias, dismantling toxicity, and demanding better
- Following the journey home to ourselves

This book won't always be neat or tidy. It won't be a quick fix. It's not meant to be. Because real, lasting change, the kind that shifts something in your soul, doesn't come from pretending everything fits into nice, neat little box.

It comes from getting *real* with yourself. With your fears, your desires, your patterns, your power.

And that process? It's messy. It's uncomfortable. It's vulnerable. It doesn't always make sense, and it's certainly not linear.

It's uncomfortable.

But it's *worth it*.

Because *you* are worth it.

Whom Is This Book For?

The short answer? *You.*

The longer answer?

This book is for all who have ever felt like they had to shrink themselves to fit in. All who have ever been made to feel like they weren't enough. All who have been told explicitly or implicitly that they had to *change* to be accepted.

It's for everyone who never saw themselves represented in their teachers, bosses, or leaders.

This book is for:

- All who exist in a workplace that wasn't built with them in mind
- Leaders who actually want to *lead*, not just manage, and create spaces where people can feel safe to be exactly who they are
- People who have lived with trauma, in the workplace or outside of it
- Black and Brown people, LGBTQ+, disabled, neurodivergent folks—all who have been marginalized, silenced, excluded, or pressured to lean to the rigidity of social norms.
- All who have ever questioned whether they belonged (spoiler: you do belong).
- For those who want to build a better future for themselves and those around them
- All who are willing to get uncomfortable, to challenge their own assumptions, to unlearn and unpack their "stuff"
- For all of us who are tired of doing things the same way simply because it feels like the only option

And yes, this book is even for people who think they don't need it. People who think they've already done the work because the work truly never ends. People who believe they have it all figured out because none of us actually has it figured out.

We're all showing up to life for the first time. This is a chance to show up together first for ourselves and then for each other.

At its core, this book is about *belonging*, not the kind that comes from fitting in but the kind that comes from *being seen*.

Fully, deeply, unapologetically seen.

I see you, and I wrote this with you in mind.

1 | Let Them

Let Them

It took me more than 30 years to understand the phrase "let them." Growing up you spend so much of your time, energy, and life trying to be likeable, to be palatable, to be tolerated.

You don't want people to think you're too much, too loud, too Black, too present. So, you shrink yourself into bite-size pieces instead of letting them see you whole.

You stay quiet instead of letting them see you angry.

You smile instead of letting them see you heartbroken.

You assimilate instead of letting them see that you are different.

The world swears it wants authenticity until you show up in full human form.

Authenticity isn't about the warm fuzzy feelings; it is about the raw unbridled human experience, and the human experience is messy, uncomfortable, and nonlinear.

Growing up in the 1990s involved a lot of bad fashion trends, low-rise denim, multitoned windbreakers, and rose-colored glasses. We were conditioned to believe that being colorblind was the future, and that education would solve all our problems. Gen-Xers spent the decade convincing my generation that ignoring race, being great at algebra, and staying quiet would solve racism. I bought into the lie and let my imagination run wild.

PBS, Sesame Street, and every show we watched taught unconditional acceptance, but they didn't teach us what to do when society fought against our individual identities. I walked through life confident that I was the same as those around me. I was sure that love and acceptance would allow people to see past the color of my skin. I convinced myself that people who experienced harrowing situations were to blame because they weren't behaving in the "right" way.

The 1990s media gaslit an entire generation to believe that our lack of access was due to our shortcomings rather than the barriers created by a society that never intended for us to succeed. We were taught to believe that kindness would heal the world, and as long as we were educated, we would be fine.

I Realized I Was Black at 25

Don't worry; the irony isn't lost on me either. This statement always feels weird for me to write, say, or even acknowledge, but it's true. Sometimes, trauma breaks us, but sometimes it makes us. I fall into the latter group. At 25, I realized I was Black and the magnitude of what that meant, and boy, was that a wake-up call.

Being biracial is *weird*. I felt like I was trapped in a body that didn't belong to me, suspended in the air, watching my flaws unfold. I grew up being told I wasn't Black enough, but I was also very obviously not white enough. I spent hours pulling at my curls in the mirror, wishing them to be straight like the white girls who tossed their hair effervescently over their shoulders. I dreamed of a life where I was as skinny as the white girls in gym class. A life where I was anything but Black. My Blackness made me feel like I was ugly because those white girls who the boys smiled at looked nothing like me. My Blackness made me feel dirty. I felt inferior, born into the wrong body. Every day, I wished I could be anyone but this person. I wanted acceptance so badly, I was willing to crawl out of my skin for it, betray my history for it, and ignore my reality for it.

I aspired to whiteness while being hyper-aware of my Black skin. I remember my parents telling me that the world was colorblind, and everyone was the same. The world no longer saw color. False. The world saw color but only chose to acknowledge "white." The only thing I saw was my Blackness, mirrored by the caricatures of Blackness seen on TV. I saw my skin as a blemish, a curse, something to be ashamed of. I searched for every way to crawl out of my own skin away from the darkness that I believed encapsulated me.

The desire to be like everyone else crept into the cracks of my deepest desires. I wanted the white picket fence, the golden retriever, the love: I wanted the life that I saw emulated in every Nick at Nite show. I felt the desire twist around my insides, convincing me that my Blackness made me undeserving of these things.

I said to myself defiantly, "I will be like them, watch me." So, I folded myself into a box that was never intended for me to fit in. I flat-ironed my hair until it broke, wore a waist trainer to look skinny, starved myself until I saw my hips wither away, denied myself love, listened to their music, and laughed at the jokes they made about me.

I am a biracial woman who grew up in the suburbs and went to boarding school followed by business school. My mom is white, and my biological dad is Black. I grew up with my mom and my stepdad, who is really my dad. They are wonderful people who always tried to do the right thing even if the "right thing" to them was actually rooted in unconscious bias and classism. I never stepped foot in a public school because my parents wanted me to have the best education that money could buy. However, they didn't know that meant keeping me from people who resembled me. They didn't realize that their idea of "best education" looked like white schools. They didn't realize they were letting *them* win, and they got exactly what society wanted: a whitewashed version of their child.

I never wanted for anything. I grew up privileged and will never deny my own privilege in this world. I never felt lucky, but I should have. I had traveled the world by the age of 10, played any sport I wanted, and always had food to eat and clean clothes to wear. My parents did what they thought they needed to do for me to be successful.

They wanted me to fit in, but their idea of fitting in meant society's idea of fitting in. My parents believed that the right education would protect their kids from racism and hate. However, education is one of the world's greatest barriers. Education is great, it's a start, but it won't solve any problems if we continue to teach watered-down versions of American history. We continue to peddle the idea of powerful white men who led a nation, when in reality they were just regular men who colonized a country that never belonged to them. This trend has continued for hundreds of years. Mediocre white men after mediocre white men have been praised in books and by the media until we believe with absolute certainty that they are better. We idolize whiteness and glorify colonization while never speaking about who actually built this country. Spoiler: It was not the founding fathers. Yet history teaches us to aspire to whiteness.

When my parents realized that I had internalized the whiteness around me, they began to panic, begging me to see my own

Blackness. I looked away. I felt betrayed by them. Isn't this what they wanted for me? My whole life, people told me, "You sound white." I never knew that was an insult. I vividly remember being excited the first time I heard those words. My subconscious was screaming, "It's working! I tricked them!" Whiteness had always been the goal in my 13-year-old mind.

How was I supposed to think anything different? I was immersed in whiteness; I was immersed in heteronormativity. All my friends were white and straight, all my professors were white and straight, everyone on TV was white and straight, and my own mother was white and straight. Success had always been painted in those brushstrokes. Business school brought more of the same. I was the girl who was often referred to as "not really Black." I used to smile so widely at that compliment. I felt important. I saw dollar signs and wedding bells every time those words were uttered by some jock who smelled like WD-40 and Natty Ice. I would toss my head back and laugh loudly at this unfunny joke, flipping my pin-straight hair behind my shoulder like those girls in elementary school, confident that was what life should feel like.

I cringe just thinking about that now. I went about life in my J.Crew loafers and Abercrombie polos, unaware there was magic hidden inside my melanin, ignoring that my true power meant experiencing the world around me as me and not the me I had conjured up from an episode of *The Hills*. I thought that I was just "the white Black girl." I didn't know what powerful felt like because I was taught I should feel weak, I should feel small, and I should step aside for whiteness to take center stage. I believed I was less than because that is exactly what the world wanted me to believe. This realization still breaks my heart because I know I am not alone in these feelings. I thought that was who I had to be. I really believed that skin color had nothing to do with who

I was or how people treated me. I even voted Republican because I was so convinced that I was "socially liberal and fiscally conservative" (ironically that doesn't exist; it's called classism). I believed racism didn't exist, and that Black people were just playing the victim. I believed that people who looked like me deserved the fates dealt to them by society. I believed we were at fault for our own marginalization.

Fast-forward 10 years, and it turns out the world sees me as Black. When I walk into a room, no matter how I sound or what I'm wearing, I'm Black, I'm queer, I am neurodivergent, I am polyamorous. I am the antithesis of what white America sees as a success. It turns out, I am powerful.

No one cares about my goddamn loafers? Huge shock.

I'm sure you're curious to know what changed for me at 25 years old. Trauma happened. But when I reflect on my life, I realize that the trauma around my Blackness started well before then. My heart and my body had to break for me to peer inside myself and see nothing but my own fears reflected back at me. For so long, I believed that my Blackness was the monster under my bed, but it was always white supremacy, lurking with blood-drenched fangs, ready to swallow me whole. I experienced blatant racism from a young age and swallowed it, internalized it, and used it to fuel my desire for whiteness. I began a relationship with a man who used my race as a form of manipulation and abuse. It wasn't his only form of abuse but his add-on once he had me living my life in fear. He wanted me to be the model girlfriend as long as I wasn't "Black." He told me I wasn't like the other Black girls he knew. I remember smiling to myself at the time, thinking I'd done something right. Little did I know that he would use this to change me, molding me into his own creation, which then he would destroy. I changed to fit a mold. His mold. I did the dishes, packed his kids' lunches, and folded his underwear. I wore my hair straight and only in approved colors. I made sure to only listen to Beyoncé and Drake when he wasn't home. I learned to not speak up because it was easier than covering black eyes and cut lips. I learned to swallow back the hurt because it was easier than telling my family what was happening inside my own home. Choking back sobs felt easier than healing out loud.

At 25, I realized that when I called the police to save me, they didn't care. They had never cared. I remember sinking to the floor, hands shoved over my eyes, bile rising in my throat at the realization that I was alone. All of the pro-police posts I'd ever shared haphazardly on Facebook had never protected me; they had not mattered. I realized as I stood in front of them, tears streaming down my face, that they would not save me.

I had to save myself.

The world collapsed around me as I realized that I hadn't gotten rid of my Blackness; I had run from it. But there it was. I had tucked the best parts of me away to preserve the way the world viewed me. I swallowed my own reality only to throw it up on my own shoes. I learned that I was the only person who couldn't see I wasn't white, that I would never be "one of them." I was always standing on the outside their circle. They were never laughing with me; they were always laughing at me. I was their best-kept inside joke. My polo shirts and phone voice couldn't save me; my straight hair went unnoticed. However, my Blackness had always been on full display.

The same thing had happened with my queerness. Desires are a funny thing. They make you feel something, and yet you end up tucking them underneath your bed because society will only judge you for them. I knew I was queer from an early age; I just didn't know what that meant. I longed for the girls in hockey uniforms in the nurses' office to smile at me, but I convinced myself I was just jealous of their athleticism. I was 13 when I realized that searching "girls kissing" on YouTube wasn't what every girl my age was interested in. So, instead, I ran my hands over my own body, fearing this was the closest I would ever come to touching a woman. I was consumed by the shame, but my lust always kept me intrigued. Even though I couldn't stop imagining soft lips on mine, I put those thoughts aside and feigned interest in boys. Queerness wasn't what society wanted from me, and that's not what my friends wanted from me, so I closed that chapter (even if I kept the YouTube tab open).

To this day, I remember the shock that shook through my core the first time a girl gripped my hand like it was the last hand she'd ever hold. I was 18 and had never lusted after a boy. All this time, I felt broken. I laid down with men because I believed it was what I was supposed to do, always darting to the shower to wash the disappointment off my body after. But when she touched me, my body lurched in desire, in confusion, and, more important, in necessity. She kissed me deeply and held me all night, and I still woke up in the morning and said, "We're just friends; this is what friends do, right?" I spent the rest of the day wondering, "Is that what it's supposed to feel like? Am I supposed to enjoy it the way I did?" No amount of showering could wash away the memory of her hands on my body. Her hands were imprinted on me, and I could still feel them as I sat down next to my boyfriend at dinner.

If you ask my mother, she will tell you she always knew I wasn't straight. The only person I was hiding from was myself. At 25, I saw the real me in the mirror. I was broken, bruised, and lost. I was unsure of my own identity, my own voice, my own heart. I stood in the shower, scrubbing my skin viciously. I was trying to wash the hate off me. Who was I without my white counterpart, the part of me that I carried in my back pocket when I needed to be taken seriously? I changed my look, changed my hair. Red hair, pink hair, blue hair. I couldn't wash it off and realized this was me. This person, these lived experiences, this skin—this was me.

That's when it finally dawned on me. I'd been showing up Black this whole time, but I was simultaneously trying to hide it. I let the shame consume me and never let myself see the reality of who I was looking at in the mirror. I had pushed my trauma so far down that I didn't see it as trauma. I saw it as the consequences of my Blackness, my queerness, the parts of me I deemed as broken. I spent 25 years being someone else to fit into boxes. Boarding school boxes, business school boxes, boxes for boys, boxes for bosses. Smile more, keep your voice down, laugh at their unfunny jokes, cover your tattoos. I was someone else for far too long, and I wasn't going to be that anymore.

At 25, I learned that I was not at fault for my trauma, but I was at fault for the pain I caused because of my own colonization. Coming to terms with the trauma you have caused is harder than learning how to cope with your own experienced trauma. I learned that to heal, I had to also acknowledge the part I had played in my own dehumanization by upholding white supremacy.

As I learned this lesson, I thought it applied only to my "personal" life. I was still turning on my phone voice for work and sliding back into those loafers. I often still "played a part" at work. Every day, I would be two people; I'd wake up Black but then clock into work as a meek, docile, neutral-toned version of myself.

I remember driving home, white knuckles on the steering wheel, as I realized that work is personal. I was seething with red-hot rage. I saw how often I had worked for people who didn't give a damn about who I was as a person, as a human being. They saw me as a Black stock photo. They'd slap me on their career site or on their "women in tech" panel and yell from the rooftops, "We're diverse!" Work has always been personal. We're expected to set boundaries in our family relationships, friendships, and casual relationships, so why the hell not at work?

I'm Still Black at Work. I'm Still Queer at Work. I'm Still Me at Work

I am often asked, "Why do you talk about your Blackness out loud? Why are you telling us about being queer?" Our identities follow us wherever we go, whether it is at work, to the grocery store, or to see friends. Work is the one place where we are supposed to pretend that our identities are sweaters that we take on and off. Imagine if that were the case?

> "BRB, Karen, I am going to put my Blackness in my cubby for the day!"
> "BRB, Chad, Just gotta tuck my rainbow in my trunk."

Would that make them more comfortable? Would they feel soothed to know that I was letting my humanity slip through my fingertips? For so long, our Blackness has been centered around the comfort of others. Historically, business leaders have danced around conversations centered on identity. They may be viewed as "political" or "offensive," but it is irresponsible to opt out of viewing the human experience from a holistic lens.

There is privilege in being able to opt out of the conversations that make some people uncomfortable. I refuse to opt out any longer, for myself and for other people who navigate the world as I do. I will no longer opt out of my Blackness to protect the comfort of white men and women who cringe at the idea that they may be ahead simply because the system was made for them to do so. I will no longer dance around explaining my family or pretending that I don't have two partners. I will not dance around my queerness to make everyone in the room feel I am palatable. We do not get to "opt out" of our Blackness, our queerness, or any other identity we hold. We are all of these things every day, no matter where we go.

My Blackness often precedes me, and it is the first thing people know about me. We do not get to opt out of the pain, fear, or trauma, and I am done letting others opt out of the truth. Opting out of reality has only protected white mediocrity. Our society was built on it. For more than 400 years, Black people, brown people, queer people, neurodivergent people, and people who dared to step off the line have been viewed as "less than" regardless of the magic we have provided the world, from slavery to segregation to voter suppression to being murdered while sleeping in our own bed. During this time, we have also continued to praise white mediocrity, while the livelihood of white people was and continues to be built on the backs of people of color.

Systems built by mediocrity will only serve mediocrity. I was recently accused of stealing jobs from "white women" because I am Black. People truly believe that affirmative action is the reason Black men and women get hired, not because we are better suited for the job. It is why hiring managers will still push back against diversity and say, "I just want the best candidate," conditioned to believe that the best talent is white. Yet whenever we talk about our existence, about our realities, a corporate America Karen starts screaming about "leaving politics out of work." Identities wouldn't need to be political if politics didn't determine how we navigate the world. What a privilege it must be to never have had politics play with your sense of safety and security.

The truth is that our identities impact us at work, and experiences that affect our personal lives also affect our work lives. We are shaped by our lived experiences, and those experiences play a part in how we view ourselves and our success. The human experience is messy, and that mess doesn't stop when we clock in.

We have been taught that we must water ourselves down to be worthy of taking up space in the corporate world. We are not less worthy of employment, advancement, and leadership because of our own traumas or who we are. This book is a roadmap to claiming our identity and shows how authenticity shows up differently in each of our personal narratives. We should be the authors in our own stories instead of allowing society to dictate the plot.

Our Stories Matter

Kimberlé Crenshaw said, "We must begin to tell Black women's stories because, without them, we cannot tell the story of Black men, white men, white women, or anyone else in this country. The story of Black women is critical because those who don't know their history are doomed to repeat it." The power of Black women isn't going anywhere, but we live in a country that will try to make us disappear. Black women continuously show up and show out for this nation, and yet we are met with hate, violence, and dismissals. I am no stranger to these behaviors. None of us are.

Black queer women have always been collateral damage in the fight for a better world. We are treated as if we are disposable. We are not disposable, I am not disposable, the next generation is not disposable. The more powerful Black women become and the more the world recognizes the power of our magic, the more danger we are in. In 1962, Malcolm X famously said, "Black women and girls are the most unprotected group in America." This still rings true. We are not safe, and this is not new. Black women are killed at a higher rate than any other group in the United States. A report done by Georgetown University showed that Black women who report abuse are less likely to be believed because Black women and girls are not seen as "innocent." This perception starts in childhood and follows us throughout our adult lives.

Breonna Taylor was murdered in her bed while she slept, and white America has still chosen to place blame on her, to blame her dating choices. Sandra Bland was murdered by police, and white America chose to blame cannabis and a psychotic break. As I write this, 48 Black women have been fatally shot by police since 2015. How many of us will become martyrs for white America's guilt before they realize that we are not the problem? How many of us will become hashtags before white America stops fearing our power? People keep saying they're tired of hearing about "race." We are tired of our Black skin being a threat to our own humanity for no other reason than the fear and entitlement of white people.

I am tired of having to prove that my life is valuable and that I deserve to survive encounters with white people. I am tired of having to hold my breath when I drive by or next to police officers. I am tired of turning on the news and seeing faces that resemble my own on the other side of the screen beside a police officer's mugshot. I wish for a day when it is no longer acceptable to watch the murder of Black people live streamed on our TVs. Trauma porn has been so prevalent in our culture that society has become numb to the murder of Black folks while our hearts are constantly stuck in our throats, our realities frozen every time the phone rings.

I am tired of making the world comfortable when I should let them sit with that discomfort the same way I sit with fear.

We are tired.

We are shaking tables and breaking barriers, but we must also break the barrier that is fear, and we cannot do that without accountability and justice. We want the same rush to justice that we see for white murder victims. We want the same humanity we see for mass murderers who are handheld and served Burger King when taken into custody.

Where was that humanity for Breonna, Sandra, or the all of the other Black women murdered by police?

They deserved to be here. They deserved to come home to themselves and their families. We must exile racism from our communities and dismantle the system. If we cannot, we can expect to sit on a never-ending carousel of heartbreak, trauma, and mediocre white men running things. History has proven to repeat itself unless you change the narrative. We have to change the story, alter the plotline, and recast the protagonist.

I wrote this book with you at the forefront of my mind.

We have a story that shapes how we show up in the world.

Our stories may not be the same, but we live parallel. I can feel our footsteps walking down these same halls. We deserve a relationship with ourselves, our true selves, not the self that society has pushed on us. We should not have to dim ourselves for paychecks, lovers, or the world. I have spent years cultivating my relationship with myself, shedding the skin of society, and dismantling the box *they* wanted to put me in.

This is a coming home story because it is never too late to come home to yourself.

You deserve to call yourself home.

The protagonists are the people who this world was built on. The antagonists must be those who intentionally protect white supremacy to save themselves. The protagonists are the Black women working 1 year, 8 months, and 16 days just to collect the same pay check as the white man sitting next to them. The protagonist is the Black man who just wants to survive his next traffic stop. The protagonist is the trans woman coming out to her boss. The protagonist is the gay couple holding hands as they grocery shop. It is the Asian man walking home from the grocery store. It is the Muslim woman taking her kids to school.

We all deserve humanity.
We all deserve safety.

We deserve to be truthful with ourselves about our needs, our wants, and our desires. We want to no longer have our lives valued on a sliding scale. However, let me be clear: Nothing will shut us up or shut us down. We will continue to take our space and ensure the generations after us know that there will never be a space they don't belong in. Most importantly, we will fight to ensure their safety.

We are writing this story, and we will not be erased from history this time.

The protagonist will no longer look like another unremarkable white face. We are the glue that holds the universe together, we are not fragmented, we are whole.

I will not water myself down in order to be palatable.

Breonna Taylor is the protagonist.
Elijah McClain is the protagonist.
Sandra Bland is the protagonist.
George Floyd is the protagonist.
Ahmaud Arbery is the protagonist.
Sonya Massey is the protagonist.

The protagonist looks like me, like you, like us.

People will make you the antagonist in their false story about you—let them. That's their story. Just make sure that you are the protagonist of your own story.

2 | Be You, for You

The "Right Way" to Be

I practiced my phone voice over and over until I sounded like the women on TV. If I just sounded the part, no one would know I'm Black during a phone screen. My voice and résumé had the masses fooled, but the double take when they met me in real life never hurt less.

I sounded prim, proper, unassuming. I spent almost my entire life learning how to blend in, how to go unnoticed, and how to become the smallest version of myself. Society tells us there is a "right way" to be. A right way to be Black, a right way to be queer, a right way to be a woman.

It seems as if the right way to be anyone was to lean in as close as you can to being a straight white man. We have been duped into believing that success looks like a white man in a well-tailored business suit.

These notions are drilled into us from all directions and from the time we can consume information. From the moment we are able to talk, we are asked to quiet our voices. From the time we are able to recognize who we are, we are told we must change, we must be different, we must be acceptable.

The Microchanges of Code-Switching

The ways we change are often subtle; they are microchanges, so small that we decide they cannot be a big deal, but how many little changes does it take before you become unrecognizable to yourself? The changes may start like changing your voice, your clothes, or your hairstyle to become more palatable by a group, whether it's at school, at work, or while dating.

This is called *code-switching*. When code-switching was first given a name by Einar Haugen in the 1950s, it was used to describe those who switch between language and dialects seamlessly. However, over time, it has been studied and used to talk about people from different cultures and backgrounds using it as a means of finding acceptance among cultural or social groups.

In 2019, Ida Harris wrote the article "Code-Switching Is Not Trying to Fit in to White Culture, It's Surviving It." In this article she reminds us that code-switching is a means of survival and not a fun game that we play to get people to like us. Code-switching is how many of us get through work, through police interactions, and through life. It is not a fun, whimsical initiative but something that is often required of us by society and patriarchal systems.

Removing "Professional" from Our Vocabulary

Oftentimes, when I speak about code-switching, people ask me, "Isn't that just called being professional?" We have been sold a lie that "professionalism" is just acting like we are someone we aren't, and if you cannot be that person, then you aren't worthy of success.

I stopped using the word *professional* many years ago because I learned that it was not created to represent people who looked like, lived like me, or loved like me. Professional was used to force people to lean into the idea that success has a mold. You do not have to look, live, or exist a certain way to be worthy of success.

White supremacy has paraded professionalism as a way to gate-keep marginalized identities from generational wealth and success. The word *professional* has been used to ensure that corporate America still has control over how Blackness looks, acts, and sounds. If you need me to sound or look a certain way to view me as a valuable team member or human, that isn't "professionalism." That's just racism in a three-piece suit.

People make assumptions about who we are based on how we look every day; people view the world through stereotypes, media, and bias. We shouldn't have to look a certain way to be treated with respect. I recently was shopping in Boston, and I was in a designer store looking for a new purse when a sales woman walked up to me to inform me that "We don't have a sales section." She assumed based on how I looked that I didn't belong in that store.

Not only do I have to look a certain way to work, I have to look a certain way to spend my own money? Absolutely not.

Oftentimes, I am asked, "What does 'professional' look like?" Every time, I roll my eyes before responding, "Not like me." I reply that way by design. A couple of years ago, someone asked my mother when I was going to move out and get a job. When my mom explained that I worked and lived in Austin, the woman said, "I just assumed, you know, because of the tattoos and the hair and stuff… ."

Stop assuming that success has to mirror the images of white men in suits you see on TV. Success looks like me. Success looks like you. Success is not binary.

The word *professional* was never intended for people like us. We were never the prototype, and I am okay with that. I do not want to be a muted version of myself when I exist in so many colors, and I want the same thing for you. You are your own prototype.

The word *professional* is why women felt like they had to be quieter and smile wider in order to gain respect.

The word *professional* is why so many queer folks pretend they're cis/hetero at work, because too often it is self-preservation.

The word *professional* is why people unlove themselves from nine to five. We pretend to be someone we're not, just to survive capitalism. The word *professional* harms all of us. It is rooted in white supremacy, heteronormativity, and bias.

By continuing to use it, we are telling our people that their worth is linked to their ability to hide their identity in cis, hetero, and white spaces. We are telling our people that their value is linked to pretending to be someone else. We are telling our people that their ability to succeed is inherently linked to how well they can shape-shift in white spaces.

Redefining Success—Today

We will no longer argue the validity of people's identities, but we will argue the validity of preconceived biased standards. Today is a great day to unpack the idea that successful looks, sounds, or loves a certain way.

Today is a great day to examine the thoughts and feelings you have about yourself and those around you and how those show up in your interactions at work and in life.

Ask yourself:

- Do I show up this way because it feels required of me, or is this who I am?
- Do I make judgments on people's lives based on how they look or sound?
- What biases am I holding onto because it is more comfortable than acknowledging harm I may have caused?

No one should have to hide to feel safe or to feel valuable. They tell us success is out of reach, and when we believe them, we make it our reality. They have convinced us that we must be like them to find success like them.

Instead, find success like you, and it will be that much sweeter.

Code-Switching As Self Preservation

For as long as I could remember, I wanted to be liked. Don't we all? We want to find and build community, we want to find love, we want to be popular. At least we think we want these things. Especially in the day and age of the Internet, we are conditioned to believe there is nothing more important than being liked, and we chase the dopamine that comes with that.

Growing up, I was always the weird kid, the one who played with bugs and wore baggy sweatpants at every chance available. In the seventh grade, on a field trip, a boy came up to me smiling and laughing and asked me on a date. I had never been asked out before, and I beamed at the chance. Before the yes was fully out of my mouth, he ran back to his friend laughing—he had asked me out on a dare. I decided in that moment that I didn't want to be the weird kid anymore. I wanted to be anyone but me, I wanted to be liked, and in that moment, I decided that I would become whoever I needed to be to be liked.

In high school, I switched schools and reinvented myself. Straight hair, polo shirts, loafers, sequins: all of the things that screamed boarding school preppy. I leaned as close as I could to whiteness because I believe in order to be liked, I had to be white. I held on to that notion for a decade. The longer I held onto it, the deeper the self-hatred and anti-Blackness grew within me.

I convinced myself that there was a right way to be Black, and I viewed anyone else who existed differently than me as "doing it the wrong way," but what I really felt was a pang of jealousy. I was jealous of the women who lived their truth and didn't care about the consequences. I was 20 years old and collecting loafers because I wanted to be liked.

Breaking Up with Code-Switching in My Personal Life

In college, I started dating a man who would change the entire course of my life, and in the moment, it wasn't in the good way. He was a racist, an abuser, and an all-around terrible human, but I was too blind to see it. I was caught up in him "liking me." It would take years for me to realize that he never liked me; he fetishized me.

In the three years that we were together, he would spend much of his time berating me for being Black, shaming me for not being thin, and highlighting all of my insecurities over and over. By the time we broke up, the sight of myself made my skin crawl. I was so far from the girl who wore oversized sweats and looked for bugs. I was unrecognizable.

To add salt to the wound, when we broke up, our break up went viral, and I mean buzzfeed viral. My mom called me to inform me they were talking about my breakup on XM radio. A video of him verbally abusing me and calling me racial slurs had spread like wildfire online. I was mortified, and the Internet is forever. As I read the comments on the videos, every comment was about me being Black. The one thing I had run from for the last 15 years was the only thing anyone noticed about me.

I was forced to have a very public, very loud, very swift reckoning. It was then that I promised myself to find a way back to me, to spend time figuring out who I was, and to forgive who I had been. I committed to being exactly who I needed to be with my friends, my family, and my future partners.

Code-Switching as a Second Job

So, I broke up with code-switching in my personal life but was it for good? Of course not because I had split myself in half. There was real me and work me, and work me was still code-switching like it was a second job. So many of us have two jobs: our actual job and the job of pretending to be someone else.

Code-switching can look different for everyone:

- How you talk
- What you talk about
- How you dress
- How you behave

For me, it was a combination of all of these things. I was always hyper-aware of how the people around me at work viewed me. I was often the "only" in my work spaces, and it felt like I had to be the representative for Blackness. I felt like I always had to be on my best behavior, not only for myself but for those who would follow after me. I didn't want to be the reason they were treated poorly. What I didn't realize was that I did more harm than good by pretending cultural groups can exist as a monolith.

I thought that I had a work me and a personal life me, and I failed to recognize how one impacted the other, because they are actually just one person. Our personal lives and our work lives bleed together because the things that impact our personal lives inherently impact our work.

For many, it is a new concept to think about how differently we show up in different spaces. However, for those who carry marginalized identities, we have always been aware of the boundaries of our realities and how to package ourselves as palatable, but just because we are good at pretending our realities don't exist doesn't make it true.

Societal and personal trauma often weigh on us like the paperweight sitting atop my taxes. The weight holds it down, but I know they're there. We cannot hide from ourselves, but we still try. That's what I did. I straightened my hair until I burned the ends off, I changed my voice, I shopped at stores that I saw marketed to the likeable girls. I was a chameleon and a good one at that. For so long, I was convinced that I could costume my Blackness from my bosses and peers. I thought if I just worked hard enough and blended in, I would be able to grow in my career. What I forgot was that no matter how hard you try to outsmart white supremacy, it bites you every time.

For many of us, code-switching at work is the second language we are fluent in. I could turn on my work voice with ease, pronouncing words in a way that sounded unnatural in my head and adding words that I would never use in conversation at home.

We spend so much time running from ourselves because we are taught to believe we are our own worst enemies. We are taught that success is a painting that is painted in predetermined brush strokes; you have to blend in.

The Wake-Up Call About Code-Switching in My Work Life

Even after I had broken up with code-switching in my personal life, I could not figure out how to break up with it at work. I tried, and each time, I was met with my own internal fear. That all changed in 2018 though. I was in the process of interviewing for a new job, and I found a company I thought I loved.

Bright-eyed and busytailed, I showed up for my interview at their office, completely unaware of how this interaction would change the course of my career. As I finished the interview, they told me they were really excited about the potential of working together and wanted to send me an offer. I felt the excitement rising in my stomach until they followed their sentence up with a "but."

They said, "We want to offer you a job here, but there are some requirements you must be willing to agree to. You have to wear a skirt or dress, high heels, cover your tattoos, take out your piercings, have natural hair color, and we would prefer if you could control your hair," she said as she motioned at my curls. In the moment, I was too flabbergasted to respond realistically, so I told her I was excited to receive the offer and to start working. I left the building feeling confused because we are conditioned to be grateful when companies want to work with us as if they are doing us a favor when they are giving us the opportunity to build someone else's dream while pretending to be someone else.

On the way home, I found myself white knuckling my steering wheel as I felt a wave of anger and sadness roll over me. It was the stark realization that so often organizations want to work with us because of what we can do for them without caring about who we are and without realizing the thing that makes us so good at what we do is us.

They wanted me to change my clothes, my skin, my piercings, and my hair. They wanted me to change my "me." Frankly, that was unacceptable. That is when I recognized this important fact.

You are the secret sauce.

I remember the first time I wore my hair curly to work; it brought me an immense sense of relief, but it also brought unwanted comments, touches, and microaggressions that I was unprepared for.

Showing up wholly, in your truth, in your body, and in your identities is not without risk. Regardless of the "bring your whole self to work" trend, no one has solved the traumatic outcomes of showing up fully at work. According to the NAACP's Legal Defense Fund, 80% of Black women have felt as if they needed to change their hairstyle to be acceptable at work (https://www.naacpldf.org/natural-hair-discrimination/). We are conditioned to believe that the hair that grows out our heads is somehow representative of our ability to do our jobs.

True Inclusivity Includes All of You

Organizations tell their employees they want authenticity, but what they put in the small print is that the authenticity is conditional; it must still fit within the tiny box they have precreated for you. Authenticity isn't warm fuzzy feelings, Black History Month, or Pride. Authenticity is the full spectrum of the human experience, and the human experience is not only beautiful and full of magic, but sometimes it is also a hot blazing dumpster fire. There is duality in the human experience, yet employers are interested only in the side that makes them comfortable.

We are not stock photos to convince boards, customers, and executives these companies are diverse. Yet, that is often how we are treated. We are silent stock photos meant to represent a lie. If your organization is only as diverse as it is willing to be comfortable, I can tell you your organization may be diverse, but it is certainly not inclusive.

Inclusion includes all sides. It does not exclude the parts of people that make us uncomfortable, and it does not exclude people's heart ache, their ailments, and their issues. Inclusion sees you at 100% and opens its arms.

In the last few years, we have seen an uptick in content that reminds us that "Work is work; why do you have to bring race into it?" Well, it's because I'm still Black at work, I'm still queer at work, I am still a woman at work.

You are still you at work, all of you, not just pieces. You cannot break yourself into pieces and expect to feel whole and to know success.

We are conditioned to believe "It's not personal; it's business." However, we are sold that lie so we don't hold our organizations accountable or hold them to the same standard we hold the people in our lives.

Work is personal, full stop. You are not a robot. You do not strip yourself of your humanity each morning at 9 a.m. as you log in to Slack. You cannot take off your human sweater and store it in your cubby until 5 p.m. No one should have to trade their truth to feel worthy of a job, a paycheck, or success. Yet we are expected to trade our well-being for survival because that is why we work: survival.

How can you give your 100% to your job if you are spending so much of your day tailoring yourself to be likeable? The answer is you can't. We do better work when we feel safe to show up. Organizations drive better results when they are less focused on who we are and instead focus on how we are.

Leaders Need to Show Up for Their Organizations

I talk about breaking up with code-switching, and I want to recognize the immense privilege in that statement. Not all organizations have done the work, and many have no interest in doing the work. Not all organizations are safe. Organizations and their leadership are solely responsible for creating environments and communities that are safe havens for their employees.

Want to know what your organization can do to start fostering safety?

- The C-suite has to be willing to do the work. Inclusion and safety aren't just fun buzzwords; they require work. Organizations must be willing to acknowledge the harm they've caused previously, out loud.
- Write and enforce policies that protect marginalized communities. Policies work only if we use them.
- Representation matters at *all* levels of your organizations.
- Inclusion and equity are not just a recruiting strategy; they are not solely the job of HR and recruiting. Inclusion is a business practice.
- You cannot solve for harm with a once a year DEI seminar. This is everyday, every-person work.

As leaders, we must be willing to check our biases and understand how our expectations, communications, and practices have encouraged our teams to feel as if code-switching was necessary. This work has to start with us. So, what does that mean? Show up for you because you will show up for others in doing so.

You Don't Need Everyone Else to Like You

We are often told that if we just change our tone or smile more, more people will like us. However, you do not owe the world likeability or fake smiles. One of the hardest lessons to learn is that you do not need people to like you. Humans thrive on community, and that desire for acceptance sometimes leads us to dive deep into people pleasing.

Trust me, I get it. I am a recovering people pleaser myself. I used to jump or dance whenever the world asked. I would do anything to feel accepted or to feel validated in my own existence. But I have healed to a place where I can be intentional about who has access to me, and you can do it, too.

It can take time to fully heal from being a people pleaser and to shift your behavior to being comfortable with not centering on the comfort of others. But you can learn to show up for yourself instead of others, and it can feel like second nature. I promise it is worth it.

You are a work of art, so be intentional with who has access to your gallery.

If people do not like you, that's okay.

If people do not want to listen to you, that's okay.

If people do not want to believe in you, that's okay. Break up with your need for external validation and lean into accepting yourself, fully, wholly, and without hesitation.

If your existence bothers people, that is a "them" problem, not a "you" problem. You must heal your validation wound so the part of you that craves validation cringes at the thought of changing for the approval of others.

You need to hold the word "no" in your hands and honor it. "No" is a full sentence; you must learn to use it. You have to stop saying "yes" to things that your body is begging you to say "no" to. This is true at work, in life, and in play. Often, we are so scared of the reactions of others that we are unwilling to say "no," and we end up putting ourselves in situations that are draining, uncomfortable, and sometimes unsafe. You deserve to say "no" to people who do nothing to build you up. Stop putting time into situations where others make it clear that they do not have your well-being at heart.

Boundaries are your best friend. They might feel uncomfortable to set, but they are meant to protect you. The only people who will have an issue with you setting boundaries are those who have benefited from you having none. The people who do not respect your boundaries or value you wholly are not your people.

It is okay to walk away from people who uphold systems that harm you or who want to break you into pieces to love you. It is okay to end friendships, relationships, and partnerships when the other party doesn't prioritize your safety over their own comfort.

You Need to Like Yourself

What I've learned on my journey is that you cannot be likeable if you don't like yourself. You cannot be some version of yourself for everyone else because then you will never be you for yourself. When you tone yourself down for society, you do yourself and the world a disservice. The world deserves to know and see your truth, and you deserve to experience the world as your true, authentic self.

I am a Black AF, Queer AF, blue-haired, hella tattooed woman who snorts when she laughs and likes pineapple on pizza. I am a force, and so are you, and that force is not for everyone. Not everyone is ready for the magic that you bring into the world.

Be you, whoever that is. Live out loud, take up space, and be whoever you are meant to be. That is your right, and it is what you deserve. It is okay to be happy, and it is okay if the definition of what "happy" means changes over time. Be sure to prioritize your happiness, your safety, and your love.

You must walk into every room and know that you belong there. But you also get to decide if the room is worthy of you being there. Not every room, space, friendship, or relationship deserves us, yet so often we stay because we find comfort in complacency.

Change is scary, and so we often stay in situations that provide no benefit, drain us, or even harm us. Change is one of the hardest things we do as humans, yet it is often one of the most rewarding things, too. Change is where growth happens. If you can get comfortable with being uncomfortable, you will be unstoppable.

You must be your first priority. Get comfortable with staring at yourself in the mirror. Learn to love your own reflection and to first take care of yourself.

There are people who will never care about what you have to say.

Make sure you care about what you have to say.

There are people who will not like you no matter what you do.

Make sure you like you.

There are people who will never believe in you no matter what you do.

Make sure you believe in you.

There are people who will never show up for you no matter what you do.

Make sure you show up for you.

You are your first and longest relationship. Nurture it.

You are your first and longest home. Don't be scared to return home to yourself.

3 | Work Is Personal, Full Stop

You Aren't Two Separate People

"It's not personal; it's business." In reality, it's not business, and it's personal. Organizations hide behind the idea that they can't hurt us because it's "just business." Being at work does not protect our hearts and bodies from harm, instead, it often amplifies the harm we experience because too often we cannot escape it.

From a young age, we are taught to separate ourselves; there is a work version and a home version, and they are never to meet. But is that reality? Absolutely not. I am the same person at 5 a.m. as I am at 5 p.m. Those versions of me have met because they are one in the same.

In a world that increasingly demands performance and productivity, many of us have tried to compartmentalize our work and personal lives. We check our emotions at the door, don a professional mask, and navigate work in ways that feel detached from our true selves.

Should we really have to trade giant parts of ourselves for a paycheck? **Absolutely not.**

A few years ago, I worked with a woman. We didn't talk much but often ran into each other in the cafeteria. She worked on the service team and always seemed so bright and chipper. It was around Christmas time, and we were planning a company happy hour. I was excited to spend more time with some of my co-workers whom I didn't know as well.

When I ran into her, I excitedly asked her if she was planning on going to the happy hour. Her face immediately fell, and she looked at me in a very serious way before saying "ab**SO**lutely not." I was a bit shocked by her answer, but before I could ask her why not, she continued, "I cannot be two people every day for more than eight hours. As it is, I sit in my car at lunch so I can call my mom, use my real voice, and take off my wig. I will not be doing any more faking it after 5 p.m."

It was like a cinderblock hit me directly the face. I touched my own hair and thought of my own curated voice and realized I was also exhausted. I was faking it every day as a means of protection, and it had become so normal to me that I hadn't even noticed. I had convinced myself that a paycheck was more important than my identity and my mental health.

The reality is that work is deeply personal. It intersects with our identities, affects our mental health, and often holds the power to shape our personal stories.

Workplaces are not neutral spaces even when organizations want them to be; they are places where our beliefs, emotions, histories, and experiences interact with the systems around us. It is here that we encounter opportunities, challenges, discrimination, and growth. But it is also here that we often experience workplace trauma, from microaggressions to burnout, that can take a significant toll on our mental and emotional health. It is impossible to separate work from the personal because that trauma and burnout comes home with us.

The Full Humanity of Identity Matters

The ways in which we navigate our identities—whether racial, gendered, cultural, or social—shape how we show up at work. We cannot check these pieces of us at the door to offer our organizations a more comfortable experience. These identities are not just things we "bring with us"; they are at the very core of how we experience work, how we are treated, and how we perform.

As leaders, it is imperative that we acknowledge not only our own experiences but the experiences of those on our teams. Ignoring that we experience work, people, and situations differently will hold us back from better understanding one another and from providing our teams with experiences that they feel safe in.

Our identities are complex, multifaceted, and ever-evolving. We are people, not things; we are multidimensional and full of differences. The person I am today may be very different than the person I am in three months. Identity is fluid. How you exist ultimately influences how you see the world, how you interact with others, and how you perform in different environments. At work, this means that our racial, gender, and cultural identities as well as our socioeconomic background, sexual orientation, and other factors significantly impact our experiences.

Your experiences with your identity at work may change over time. When I first entered the job market, I wasn't out, and coming out inherently changed how I view work and how I was viewed at work. The experiences you have today may not be the same experiences you have forever, but they will permanently shape your outlook. Your experience with your identity is your own and deeply personal to you. Your experience will not mirror everyone elses' or even anyone else's.

For many, the workplace may feel like a space where they are forced to change and be a muted version of themselves to avoid discrimination and trauma. Workplace trauma is trauma, and it can manifest in many ways, such as microaggressions, exclusion, or even outright harassment. It is exhausting to be two people, yet we are forced to play a tug-of-war game with our selves between who we are and who we think we need to be to protect ourselves. Workplace trauma, whether physical, emotional, or psychological, has lasting impacts on your team's mental health, creating an environment where individuals are more likely to experience anxiety, depression, burnout, and emotional exhaustion.

How can we expect people to be successful if they are consistently stuck in fight-or-flight mode?

How can we expect people to pour from an empty cup?

Your team cannot pour into your organization if you do not pour into them.

When our people are constantly navigating these complexities—adjusting themselves to fit into a mold that doesn't acknowledge their full humanity—it is not only exhausting but also traumatic to have the realization that the "full you" is not worthy of a paycheck or to be worthy of a successful life you must be different than who you are. The impacts of this idea seep into all aspects of our lives until we believe we are not good enough, period.

This is where the power of authenticity comes into play. When we can bring our true selves to work, when we feel valued for who we are and not just what we can do, it transforms the entire work experience. As leaders we have the ability to empower people to truly show up and find confidence in their own identities and who they are.

What if work wasn't just a place we go to earn a paycheck but an environment where our identities, values, and well-being were seen? How much better would we be at our jobs if we didn't have to worry about how we were perceived? How much better do we come across when we can trust that we are safe? What better gift could we could give people than the gift of acceptance?

Managing to Denormalize Workplace Trauma

Workplace trauma is often invisible but incredibly damaging. You may have felt like you had to endure silently and just "continue on" because we have normalized the idea that work must also be the worst part of our lives, the thing we dread, the Sunday scaries.

Contrary to popular belief, work shouldn't suck, work shouldn't be the only topic you bring up in therapy, and work shouldn't be a source of pain. Unfortunately, for many, this is the case. I have worked at a few companies where crying and yelling were regular activities, and for a long time I believed they were normal.

It wasn't until much later in my career that I had the realization that work should be a place where we get to exist freely without being made to feel poorly about ourselves. Yet the media has normalized hating our jobs and our managers.

What if I told you there was a better way? If you're a manager, be the manager you wish you had when you were first beginning your career. If you're not a manager and you have options, seek out organizations or teams that provide good managers.

Think of the worst managers you've ever had. What qualities did they have that you would never want to repeat? Now think of the best managers you've ever had. What qualities do they have that you want to embody? The following table shows some common traits of the best and worst managers:

Worst Managers	Best Managers
Yelling	Owning mistakes
Shaming people	Being open to being challenged
Micro-managing	Communicating effectively but kindly
Using fear-based leadership	Being honest

If more managers were honest about the experiences they've had and how those experiences impacted them in and out of work, we would be able to move the world of work forward. We cannot move forward and do better without acknowledging our own hurt and trauma.

There is no shame in being impacted emotionally by work, but we cannot overcome it without actively moving through and acknowledging the workplace's impact on us. Spend some time with yourself to document and journal how the best and worst managers you have had have left a mark on your life.

Authenticity is not just about acknowledging who we are, but about acknowledging what we have experienced.

Many organizations, though perhaps not intentionally harmful, perpetuate environments that lead to employees suffering in silence. The power dynamics of our organizations do not allow most to feel safe coming forward with their experiences. As managers, we cannot rid ourselves of the power dynamic between us and our teams, but if we can acknowledge it, we can open up the door for safe communication.

The impact of our organizations will always matter more than the intention. Whether through systemic discrimination, toxic work cultures, or demands for constant productivity at the expense of mental well-being, trauma in the workplace has real, lasting consequences on mental health.

Isolation, Exclusion, and Burnout

Burnout is one of the most widespread symptoms of workplace trauma. It can be caused by excessive workloads, unrealistic expectations, and lack of support, and it leads to emotional exhaustion, detachment, and diminished performance. According to the World Health Organization, burnout is a syndrome that results from chronic workplace stress that has not been successfully managed. We often think of stress as it relates to deadlines, projects, and meetings, but what could be more stressful than being demonized for who you are? Burnout is characterized by feelings of depletion or exhaustion, increased mental distance from one's job, and reduced professional efficacy, and then you bring all of that home with you.

Want to know what breeds burnout? Isolation. Feeling alone in your struggles.

Isolation kills. Humans crave community; it is at the core of who we are and how we experience life. Exclusion is another common form of workplace trauma. Employees from marginalized groups often experience exclusion or discrimination based on their race, gender, sexual orientation, or other aspects of their identity. Whether overt or subtle, these acts of bias—microaggressions, lack of representation, or outright harassment—create an environment where people feel devalued and unsafe.

The mental health toll of such trauma is undeniable and well documented, so why isn't it a bigger concern for most organizations?

The constant emotional labor of navigating these hostile environments can lead to feelings of isolation, stress, anxiety, depression, and even physical health issues. This kind of trauma can be as damaging as any physical injury, yet it is often overlooked or minimized by organizations that fail to understand its impact.

These traumas may feel micro, but they are simply fractures in a much larger wound.

We see these behaviors perpetuated in hiring processes, which then dictates the environment within our organizations. Exclusionary hiring practices lead to isolation in the workplace. No one wants to be the "only one"—the pressure of being the representative for an entire community is not only stressful but can also be harmful. When you are the "only," you are burdened with feeling as if you must be on your best behavior to not spoil people's perception of your identity even though no identity group is the same or could be defined by a singular person.

Yet so many organizations believe as long as they check the box and have at least one person from whatever group is their flavor of the week, then they have done their job. Instead of hiring intentionally for diverse lived experiences, they would rather check boxes.

Trapped Between the Riddle and the Couch

Many years ago, I encountered a manager who was anything but conventional (and not in the fun way) when it came to interviewing. He used two methods to evaluate candidates: the riddle and the "couch test." On the surface, both seemed harmless enough, but when you looked a little deeper, they revealed a more insidious side of his approach to hiring.

The first method, the riddle, would catch almost anyone off guard. The manager would sit across from you, often with a smug grin and deliver a seemingly nonsensical question that had no clear answer. Something absurd like, "How many times can you subtract the number 5 from 25?" If you gave him a logical answer, something like "five times," he'd simply shake his head and say, "Wrong. You can only subtract 5 once, because after that, it's not 25 anymore." The explanation was always absurd, but it wasn't really about the riddle itself. The riddle was just a tool to gauge how you'd react under pressure; at least that's the story he fed us.

What I came to realize over time—and what I couldn't see at first—was how this riddle was a subtle barrier. And to be honest, I don't think he ever cared about the answer. He wanted to make candidates feel dumb and then use it as a way to disqualify candidates who he didn't "see fit" for the company. It was a game to him and an opportunity to play God.

And there was a pattern. **All of the Black women who interviewed with him? They all failed the riddle.** They were dismissed without a second thought. No questions about their experience, no further probing into their qualifications. Just a rejection based on a question that never had a right answer. It wasn't just bias. It was blatant racism, but because he held a seat of power, he was allowed to hire as he pleased without any recourse for the other person. According to a 2020 study by the National Women's Law Center (NWLC), Black women face the greatest racial and gender disparities in employment opportunities. Black women are hired at a much lower rate than white women even when their experience and education exceeds their counterparts.

The second method, the "couch test," was simple, but the bias ran deep. After the formalities of the interview, he'd ask you a seemingly innocuous question: "So, imagine we're at a party, and there's a couch. I want to know, would I want to sit next to you on that couch?" The idea was that, based on your personality, he would decide if you were someone he could be comfortable around, someone he would want to have a beer with, someone he would want to see outside of work. If he thought you'd get along well in personal settings, he would move you forward. But if he didn't feel the connection and think you'd be someone he couldn't talk to over a beer or a drink, then you were out. Seems harmless enough, right?

But there was nothing harmless about it. This was where the true bias took form. He'd never admit it, of course, but it was obvious that the "couch test" was never about personality or cultural fit—it was about something much more insidious. The people who were likely to fail were the ones who didn't fit his idea of whom he'd be comfortable with, his idea of what "relatable" looked like. And if you were a Black woman? It was a nearly guaranteed fail. You see, **this wasn't just about comfort—it was about whom he was willing to make space for in his world.** The lack of diversity on his team didn't happen by accident. It was a result of decisions like these: decisions masked in the guise of "fit" or "chemistry" but really about something else entirely.

This is unacceptable. When we are hiring for our teams, we must break ourselves of the pattern of needing to hire for sameness. You should not want to get a beer with all the people you work with or see them outside of work. It is actually perfectly okay to hire people you don't even like. If we only hire people who we get along with in the personal sense, then we are hiring people who are most likely pretty similar to us.

Bias Is Toxic for the Entire Organization

The more I observed the riddle-and-couch hiring process, the more I began to see how much this bias was allowed to shape the entire culture of the team and how the hiring process instilled fear in the people who worked closest to this manager, and I recognized that it was by design. I watched as talented women of color were turned away with no feedback, older folks were rejected for reasons like "culture fit," and straight white men had the red carpet rolled out for them. And what bothered me the most was that we were all so caught up in the grind of hitting our hiring metrics that no one seemed to care enough to put the dots together.

I remember one time, a Black woman, a badass customer experience manager, came in for an interview. She had all the credentials and all the experience and was an absolute delight. She had come from well-known companies and came highly recommended from someone at our organization. But when the riddle came up, she magically failed. He didn't tell us why or how or even what her answer was; he just said no. The look on my face must have been a mix of disbelief and disappointment because he looked at me and said his decisions were none of my business even though I was the recruiter working on the role. I felt that sinking feeling that I had often felt when I recognized I was being rejected because of who I am, but this time I was seeing it happen to others because they couldn't play a game stacked against them from the start.

Over time, I realized this wasn't an isolated incident. There was an unspoken pattern that anyone who didn't fit this manager's personal preferences—a certain look, a certain personality, a certain way of carrying themselves—was sidelined. He would talk about "fitting in" like it was some objective standard. But I knew better. It was about making people fit into his narrow vision of what was acceptable.

I wasn't the only one who witnessed it. Many of us in that office had noticed the same pattern of exclusion. We also felt outside of the hiring process. He made his disdain known for people who were different than him. How do you think this made anyone who reported to him feel? I didn't report to him, and it still left me feeling on edge. I eventually had the courage to bring the issues up with my direct manager. I came with notes and receipts and all of the things to back up what I was saying, and still nothing changed. I was told, "It's just the way he does things. We don't question it." It was easier to let it slide than to have the hard conversations about the harm that was being caused.

It wasn't until I was in a leadership role myself that I understood the unspoken power behind those willfully blind eyes. Bias isn't just something we passively accept; it's something we actively perpetuate when we let it slide. Many organizations would rather cause harm than to acknowledge that they have put harmful players in positions of power.

Looking back, I wish I could've explained to those candidates that it wasn't them but the system at work. It wasn't until I left that toxic environment that I realized the full scope of what had been happening and began to understand just how deeply these microaggressions and small biases ran. They had been justified by a system that didn't prioritize fairness; instead, it prioritized conformity. And as I moved through my career and started to build my own teams, I became painfully aware of the responsibility I carried, not just to be aware of my own biases but to actively work against them and to call out the biases that existed on my own leadership teams.

I've seen firsthand how small, seemingly insignificant moments can lead to profound, lasting impacts on someone's mental health. But the truth is bias doesn't just affect the person being discriminated against—it's toxic to the entire organization. The riddle and the couch test? They weren't just quirky little methods of evaluation; they were the perfect encapsulation of a workplace culture that was built on exclusion.

Checking Your Own Biases

We build harmful systems into our organizations when we are unwilling to check our own biases. Wanting to hire people you want to "sit on a couch" next to or refusing to hire certain kinds of people isn't a flex, and it isn't good leadership—it is fear. Fear of being challenged, fear of different kinds of people, fear of change.

We have biases, but we are in control of how we outsmart them and how we coach ourselves around them. Yet when we refuse to do this, we create cultures of harm within our organizations and in our teams.

Checking ourselves is one of the hardest things we can do because it requires an uncomfortable level of honesty with ourselves. It's easy to point fingers and blame others for their biases, but the real work begins when you turn the mirror back on yourself. What assumptions do you carry that you don't question? What beliefs have you internalized without ever considering where they come from? Bias doesn't have to look like hatred—it can be the quiet, invisible way we favor what feels familiar and dismiss what feels different.

We have biases, even people who are committed to equity, to inclusion, to doing better. I do this work for a living and I am not without fault or bias. But if you're not constantly checking yourself, if you're not willing to confront your discomfort and challenge what feels like "truth," then you're complicit in perpetuating systems that harm others. This isn't about being perfect; it's about being willing. Willing to unlearn, willing to grow, and, most importantly, willing to do the hard, messy work of confronting yourself before you expect to change the world around you.

When we take the time to check our biases, we're not just addressing our personal shortcomings; instead, we're creating the foundation for a more inclusive, empathetic, and effective culture within our companies and on our teams. Letting our biases go unchecked seeps into our decisions, our interactions and, ultimately, the way people feel valued by us. But when we actively confront and challenge our biases, we make space for diverse perspectives, foster true safety, and open up opportunities for everyone to thrive. It's in that willingness to self-reflect and do the hard work that we build cultures where people feel safe, seen, and heard—not just tolerated but truly respected for who they are. And when people can show up as their full, authentic selves, they bring their best work to the table.

So, checking your biases isn't just a feel-good exercise; it's a strategic move that drives innovation, creativity, and collective success.

What Is Authentic Leadership?

One of the most profound ways to shift the trajectory of workplace trauma is through authentic leadership. Leaders who embrace their own vulnerability and authenticity can create a culture where employees feel safe, valued, and empowered to bring their full selves to work. Authentic leadership isn't just about transparency; it's about creating a space where emotional and psychological safety are prioritized and where individuals are not punished for showing up as their full selves.

Too often we see leaders who share articles and attend seminars about psychological safety but never put it into practice because the idea of self-reflection can be daunting.

Leaders who model vulnerability don't just inspire trust; they create environments where vulnerability becomes an asset. Authentic leadership invites employees to be open, honest, and transparent without fear of repercussion. When leaders openly acknowledge their own struggles, mistakes, and limitations, they show that it's okay to not be perfect. This breaks down the emotional walls that often exist in hierarchical, corporate structures and encourages a more human, connected work environment.

Humanizing Leadership to Create a Better Culture

So, how can you show up in a way that positively impacts your teams?

As a leader, showing vulnerability doesn't mean airing personal details or laying bare every struggle. It's about **humanizing leadership** and creating a culture where mistakes are seen as opportunities for growth rather than failures. Human-centered teams drive trust and innovation.

Here's how leaders can model vulnerability and authenticity:

- **Being Transparent About Challenges and Failures**

  Safe leaders acknowledge that they, too, face challenges and setbacks. They're not afraid to admit when they've made mistakes, taken wrong turns, or learned the hard way. By sharing our experiences, we remind our teams that perfection isn't the standard and that mistakes are part of the journey toward improvement. Give your people space to fail. Innovation does not come from trying the same things over and over; it comes from having the space to take a risk and try something new.

  When leaders share their own struggles, it allows their teams to see that they are human too, it creates an environment where team members feel safe to do the same. We must be willing to model the behavior we expect from our teams. Vulnerability fosters connection: It allows employees to see their leaders as human beings, not just authority figures. We must be seen as more than managers, we need our teams to see us as fellow humans.

- **Embracing The Mess**

    Authentic leaders acknowledge that they don't have all the answers and that they rely on the expertise of their teams. We are winging it, and that's okay. No one knows everything, and it's time to stop pretending that we do. Start asking your teams questions and ask for their feedback; ask what they need from you and actually listen. Root your leadership style in collaboration rather than in fear.

- **Fostering Emotional Intelligence**

    The hardest thing we do as managers is manage the human element of our teams. Vulnerable leadership requires emotional intelligence. We must be able to manage and understand our own emotions while showing up with empathy for the emotions of others—at the same time. This is not easy work, especially when the emotions of our team may bump up against our own. When you are an emotionally intelligent manager, you can navigate sensitive conversations, mediate conflicts, and support team members in a way that makes them realize that you see them for who they are and not just what they can do. Safe managers also create a culture where emotional well-being is prioritized, and mental health struggles are met with compassion and care rather than annoyance and frustration.

- **Leading with Empathy**

    Empathy in leadership involves genuinely caring about the well-being of your team. It's about understanding their struggles, celebrating their victories, and being present when they need support. Leaders who show empathy are more likely to reduce workplace trauma because they create environments where employees feel seen and respected.

When you can show vulnerability and honesty, you model how to approach life and work with grace and humility. You set the tone for a supportive, trauma-informed workplace where employees feel safe enough to bring their whole selves to work.

- ■ **Encouraging Feedback and Open Dialogue**

  We must create intentional space for critical dialogue and feedback of ourselves and our management style. Although criticism doesn't feel good, it can often make us better leaders to hear what is not working. We must be willing to listen to their concerns, understand their experiences, and co-create solutions together, as a team. This kind of feedback loop helps prevent misunderstandings and promotes a culture everyone's voice gets to feel important.

Committing to Leading Authentically with Intention

When we commit to vulnerable leadership on our teams, it is a ripple that can be felt by our entire organization. Our organizations see our authenticity and are encouraged to mirror those behaviors. Safe cultures start from the top; we cannot expect individual contributors to be at the helm of our cultures. Leadership as a whole must commit to understanding themselves so they can better understand their teams.

The secret sauce for having an organization where employees are fully engaged is creating a culture f of safety and vulnerability.

It is especially true for employees who are navigating previous trauma. When traumatized employees finally gets to work with a leader who is empathetic and caring, it allows them to let their walls and down and take that first deep breath where they can say "I belong here." We can create lasting effects on those who have experienced trauma by giving them the opposite experience. We give people the space to heal when we choose to see them for who they are rather than for what they can do.

The journey to creating healthier work environments starts with you. **Full stop.**

It's easy to point fingers, blame management, or roll your eyes at the latest corporate initiative designed to check off a diversity or inclusion box. But let's get real: The power to change the culture around you is in your hands. If you truly care about the mental health of your team—and not just the performance metrics—you've got to lead from the front.

Showing up authentically isn't just some trendy buzzword. It's the foundation of everything that follows. It must be the foundation of how you lead, period. When you bring your real self to the table—flaws, insecurities, and all—you invite your team to do the same. Vulnerability isn't weakness; it's a damn superpower. It's not about exposing all your cards but about allowing space for people to show up as they are. And that's where psychological safety starts to flourish. When people feel safe to speak their truth and express the full range of their emotions without fear of retaliation or judgment, **your team transforms** and so does the team's productivity, loyalty, and mental health.

So, what's the catch?

This isn't a one-off act of kindness or a "good vibes" initiative that fades when the next quarter rolls around. You can't care about this work only when your company is crunching numbers. This work must continue when the economy sucks, when you're going through organizational changes, and when work isn't all rainbows and butterflies.

This is an everyday commitment. It's not enough to tweet about mental health or slap a few words on a mission statement. The real work requires hard conversations in the mirror. But if you want to be the change, you've got to check yourself—constantly. Bias, judgment, assumptions—they don't just vanish because you've acknowledged them once. It's a continual process of self-reflection, feedback, and growth. And don't expect the people around you to do all the heavy lifting when it comes to creating this culture.

This starts with you.

I refuse to sugarcoat it: Workplace trauma is real, and it's deeply ingrained in how organizations function. It's deeply ingrained into use because capitalism has convinced us that the trade-off for groceries and rent must be paid in battle wounds.

Systems of oppression, toxic power dynamics, and unacknowledged microaggressions do not just magically disappear when you decide to be a "good manager" for the day.

Are you a good manager when you're angry? Are you a good manager when you're scared? Are you a good manager when everything is not going your way?

If you want to create a truly healthier work environment, you need to go deep. Acknowledge the harm that has been done, whether you were directly responsible or not. Admit that your company's culture may have been built on unhealthy dynamics, even if it was unintentional. No more excuses or sweeping things under the rug. No more running from the hard conversations.

It ends with us.

The trauma your team carries with them—whether from burnout, discrimination, or invisible wounds—doesn't just vanish because you slapped a wellness program and a pizza party into the mix.

And let's get one thing straight: Just because people don't voice their trauma doesn't mean it isn't there. People will smile, will meet their deadlines, send their silly little emails and will pretend everything is fine while silently battling the weight of all the trauma they have experienced over their careers. *They're holding it together for now but at what cost? They're holding it together but for how long?*

If you're not creating a space for people to be honest about their lived experiences, you're contributing to the problem.

Whether it's a toxic culture that prioritizes productivity over well-being or a pattern of dismissing mental health as an "individual problem," your silence or inaction is part of the trauma.

Leaders, it's time to get uncomfortable. **You cannot be afraid to rock the boat and flip some tables.** Start challenging the status quo even when it feels safer to maintain the "just keep your head down" mentality. The truth is, your team is watching you, not just for your vision or your leadership but for how you show up as a human being, how you show up for other human beings. When you choose authenticity over the "perfect leader" façade, you create space for others to step into their own truth.

If you want a culture where mental health is taken seriously, where vulnerability is celebrated and not punished, where people are empowered to be their authentic selves without fear of judgment or retaliation, then you will need to lead the charge. The work isn't easy, it isn't going to be quick, and it never ends, but the payoff is a team that gets the experience that they deserve.

It's going to be messy, it's going to be uncomfortable, and it will stretch you in ways you didn't expect but it will be worth it. So, don't wait for permission. Don't wait for a perfect moment. The future of work isn't some idealized space where everything is perfect and everyone is kumbaya-ing in harmony. The future of work is about radical honesty, real vulnerability, and unapologetic authenticity. If you're not willing to lean into the discomfort of change, then step aside and let someone who's ready to lead in the twenty-first century take the reins.

The future is already here, and it's time to step up, take responsibility, and lead with intention.

4 | Rewriting History

The Problem with Good Leaders

I'm throwing away the phrase "good" leadership. Don't throw the book down yet; stick with me. We are so quick to shove the word "good" in front of everything, forgetting that it creates a binary. Good is not enough, good is not intentional enough, good does not move us forward. Like so many things in this world, it is not that simple.

We don't need "good" leaders; we need impactful leaders. We need safe leaders. We need leaders who are capable of saying they are sorry. We need leaders who can lead through catastrophe, chaos, and turmoil. We need leaders who are human, and humans are not binary.

Leadership isn't for everyone, and that's okay. Capitalism has us fooled into thinking we must be managers, leaders, and CEOs. We are taught from very young ages that to earn more, to be worth more, and to become more valuable, you must be a manager. We see it on the sitcoms we watch growing up, we hear it from our families, and then we have the constant push of capitalism knocking at our doors.

Fear-Based Leadership

Leadership and management should be career paths for people who truly care about how they elevate the humans around them, yet it has become a merciless field of people who thrive in power and will cause harm in the name of a power trip. Power is a hell of a drug—just watch the news. People chase power, and it has been what he have done for centuries. History has taught us time and time again that we can grasp power if we can make others feel fear.

Unfortunately, this methodology was not lost on people entering the work force. Fear-based leadership is common, even though it is proven that it doesn't work. At least 5% of the world's workplace population (13 million people) have PTSD induced by their working conditions according to Workplace Options. Our minds and bodies cease to function effectively when we're in fight-or-flight mode. They rely on safety to perform well. Yet so many leaders do not know how to lead except through fear.

In 2021, Desmond Hardy tweeted a viral tweet asking the public about their experience with workplace trauma and PTSD, and the response was astounding. He asked, "Has anyone ever had toxic workplace PTSD? Like, the chime sound of an incoming email evokes your 'fight, flight, or freeze response?' Just me?" It gained more than 50,000 likes and 6,000 responses from people who felt seen by his callout. So many of us have experienced toxic workplaces, but we live in fear of speaking out about it. It's likely that you or someone you know has experienced at least a few of the following situations:

- Being talked down to, insulted, or patronized
- Being shouted at
- Having someone get in your face or personal space
- Having a manager publicly shame or humiliate you in front of the entire team

- Having a manager from a different team try to control you as if you are on their team
- Being intimidated until you start second-guessing your decisions
- Being unfairly treated due to sexism, racism, homophobia, transphobia, ableism, ageism, classism, or belonging to any other marginalized identity
- Being inappropriately touched or physically threatened
- Being so mistreated that you cry at work or at home
- Being mistreated to pressure you into quitting
- Being abused by croneys of people in power
- Having a manager or human resources department enable the person who is mistreating you
- Having the organization protect its image and managers over the safety of its team members

These experiences are unacceptable. There has to be a better way.

Please raise your hand if you have been personally victimized by fear-based leadership.

I hate to break it to you, but having the Sunday Scaries isn't normal. We shouldn't feel dread the night before we return to work. Work should be a place where we come to do what we need to do and then log off and continue on with our days, but when fear-based leadership is in the mix, that fear returns home with us. You cannot compartmentalize those fear-based emotions and experience them only from 8 a.m. to 5 p.m. (or whatever your working hours are). We hold our experiences in our bodies and in our daily lives. (And that goes both ways. We carry the experiences from our daily lives to work, too.) The stress of working at a job that makes you feel fear or makes you doubt yourself can and will be detrimental to you on an emotional, physical, and professional level.

Even years later when I think about the workplaces that I have been in that have traumatized me, I can feel the weight in my chest, the familiar turning of my stomach, and it all comes rushing back. Trauma doesn't leave us even when we heal. We remember what it feels like to be right back in the cubicle, in that meeting, in that moment.

I remember a time when I worked for a tech company early in my career; it was my first senior role, and I was excited to finally have broken into an industry I long admired. I spent the morning in all of my necessary training and getting access to the multitude of different tech stacks I would be utlizing, but my afternoon was free to do what I wanted, and I wanted to get started. I had been given all of my open roles, their requirements, and candidates, so I started dialing. A few hours into my day, a male VP comes up and grabs my phone from my hands and asks me what I think I'm doing. Stunned, I let him know that I was calling candidates to set up phone screens. Slamming my phone down he says, "I didn't tell you that you could do that." This man was not my boss and was not on my team; he was just a guy who shared my cubicle block with a much higher title than me.

Every day after that, I second-guessed picking up the phone, sending an email, or even making decisions without him knowing even though he didn't need to. From that day forward, he made it a point to ensure that he was involved in my day-to-day, often shaking his finger in my face, insulting my candidates and myself, and watching my every move. He knew what he was doing; it was by design.

The day I finally quit, I was relieved but a little sad to leave a company I had come to love because of one manager who didn't even manage me. I gave my notice to my manager and let her know that my last week would be in two weeks and I'd spend that transitoning anyone in process to my recruiting partner.

Well, wouldn't you know, even in my exit he wouldn't allow me that kind of control. Once he got word that I had put in my notice, he waited until my manager had gone to lunch, and he pulled me into a room with a woman who had moved from his team to HR with no experience other than he referred her. He told me that he found my presence to be distracting, and he was making my last day that day.

He proceeded to have me escorted to our cubicle row, and he stood over me inspecting every item that I packed to ensure it wasn't company owned while the entire office watched silently (I suppose that is the downside of these open floor plan trends). I could feel the embarrassment from my head to my toes as I turned every shade of red you could think of. I spent the rest of the day crying and answering text messages asking why I'd been fired. He didn't do it for any other reason than to bask in the fact that he could, and he found power in making me feel small.

Trauma is not the price we should have to pay to receive a paycheck. I'd love to be able to say I think he is an outlier, but he isn't. For many, he is a regular manager, because so many of them wield their power like a weapon, especially for those who hold marginalized identities; they use their privilege to create harm.

During my time there, I reported the behavior, I kept receipts, I even documented every time he made a racist remark about a candidates, and I did all of the things that I could find when I Googled my predicament. I documented and documented, and it didn't matter. Why? Organizations who do not care about their people will always protect the ones who do their bidding. In this case, he was the CEO's college roommate, and to this day he is employed as a C-suite executive with nothing else on his résumé except "Backpacker" and white dude.

He still looks at my LinkedIn at least once a week; I hope he has learned I don't let anyone make me feel small now.

So, if we've all experience fear-based leadership, why do we keep continuing to do it? Why do bad managers create more bad managers instead of managers who want to break the mold? Why are we still trying to convince organizations of the value of safety? It's simple: power pays. Organizations are too interested in lining their pockets instead of doing the right thing. Around 2020, many organizations signaled there was going to be a shift in how they felt about their people, and they did a good job at fooling us, but so much of it was smoke and mirrors. It was a shift for their customer and investor bases, not a shift for humanity; in other words, it was a shift with dollar signs on the end of it.

Since then, we have seen organizations retract, reverse, and completely throw out their commitments to equity and safety in the name of "civility." We don't need more civility; we need more real conversations about how people experience work and the world around them. We need organizations that care about the humans who build their dreams, and we need managers who care about the humans they are leading. Giving humans the space to feel safe in their environments shouldn't be controversial.

Becoming Better Leaders

So, how do we change our organizations to truly care about their people? We become the leaders we wish we had. When I think of my role as a leader, it falls into three categories: growth, safety, and space.

- I manage my teams in a way where my intent is always to grow them to their potential and leave all individuals more equipped than when I met them.

- I try to give them the safety to be exactly who they need to be and know that their needs will shift over time and may even be different from day to day.
- I do my best to provide them the space to fail.

Our ability to lead should be human-first and safety-centered. Therefore, we must be willing to bare our humanness to our teams. Showing up human-first instead of accolade-first is scary. We are taught to rely on our skills, résumé, and grit rather than who we are. Let's flip that narrative. We cannot expect our teams to feel safe if we are unable to show them that we are also human.

Human-First Leadership

Want to be a better leader? Always strive to do better. Practice doesn't make perfect; it makes progress. Move the future of work forward by centering on humanity.

Humanize Your Teams

The people on your teams are just like you. They experience the world in multitudes, and their day-to-day changes as often as yours does. Humans experience an array of emotions and experiences over the course of their lifetime, and all of this impacts how they show up to work. Give them grace and space to experience life as it happens. We may never know the entirety of the inner workings of someone's life, but we can have empathy for the mess of the human experience. No one will be able to be on 100% every day, and we must be willing to honor that.

Humanize Yourself

You are not invincible. If you expect vulnerability from your teams, you must be willing to be vulnerable yourself. As managers, it's easy to talk ourselves into believing that we must be strong, perfect, and solemn at all times. That is not reality; if we want our teams to be open with their experiences, then we must be willing to be vulnerable with our own. First, we must be willing to be vulnerable with ourselves before we are able to be vulnerable with anyone else. That is the hardest part. You do not owe the world perfection. You do not owe the world emotionless leadership. Your emotions, your experiences, and your voice is what makes you a strong leader; do not shrink yourself to appear stronger.

Human existence is many things, but the one thing it is not is perfect. We mess up, we get it wrong every once in a while, and we don't know everything. That is okay, but let's start owning it. It is okay to say to your teams that you do not have the answer to something or that you got something wrong. If we want to build teams of self-aware leaders, we have to be willing to be self-aware with ourselves.

Power Through Vulnerability

When was the last time you had a hard conversation with yourself in the mirror? To be vulnerable with others, we first must be willing to be vulnerable with ourselves. So many of us avoid having the inner conversations because we let shame and ego float to the surface. Somewhere along the lines we were taught that having needs was shameful. (Abraham Maslow definitely would not approve of this development.) The Internet is swimming with content that pushes hyperindependence, raging egoes and ways to avoid dealing with your emotions. Stop listening to the Internet; it's not always right.

If you want to be an impactful leader, peer, or friend to others, you have to be willing to be those things to yourself first. You will meet yourself over and over again over the course of life, and each version of you will have different needs. Get to know them. You can't continue to run away from the reality of your needs forever; you must meet yourself where you are.

Practice getting to know yourself the same way you would get to know a peer or co-worker. You can start by journaling or asking yourself these questions in the mirror:

- What are you feeling right now in this moment?
- What can I do to make your life easier?
- What do you need to feel seen?
- Are you okay?

Write down your answers. They won't always feel good, and that is okay. You can also watch how they change and evolve over time throughout your life.

You cannot expect yourself to show up for others when you are unwilling to even meet your own gaze in the mirror.

There is power (the right kind) in vulnerability. Showing your true self to your teams is an act of courage, and one that many leaders are unwilling to take. I intentionally make it a point to be vulnerable with my teams, not because it is easy but because I want them to know they are safe to show up there. You don't have to share the details of your personal life, but I make it a point to take my mental health days, to acknowledge the events of the world, and to admit my faults and weaknesses.

You Don't Know Everything, and That's Okay!

There is a primal urge as a manager to feel you must be smarter, more powerful, and better equipped than everyone on your team. It's a lie you're sold to continue to promote fear-based leadership. You do not have to know everything, and it's actually impossible for you to know everything; anyone who tells you otherwise is lying. As a leader, your job is to lead, and the first rule of leadership is honesty. Be willing to admit when you don't know an answer. Be willing to admit when someone on your team knows more than you. Our goal as leaders should be to help our teams become better than we are. Oftentimes, our egos get in the way of that. Our egos tell us that when we allow someone else to shine, they become our competition. Our teams are not our competition; instead, they should be our motivation.

In my time as a coach and consultant, I have often heard managers say that they don't want to manage people who are smarter than them or who have more earning potential than them. I once had a leader who told me they were unwilling to lead anyone if they made more than they did. This role was a sales role, and his team earned a commission—he said it was unfair for him to be giving them his knowledge only for them to turn around and make more money.

That isn't leadership; that is power, and the desire for it. Continually grasping for power is your ego speaking, not your vulnerability. When we fear our own vulnerability, we begin to rely on our ego to guide us. True vulnerability requires putting your power down and trusting yourself as someone who is capable of leading through empathy rather than fear. Impactful leadership isn't about competition or trying to see who can kick who off the proverbial corporate ladder. Safe leaders should want to have people on their teams who can teach them. Leadership is not about your power but about your ability to build safety and community within your teams.

Most importantly, be willing to say you're sorry when you mess up or get something wrong. There is power in showing your faults: No one is perfect, and that is okay.

People Perform Better in Safe Environments

The old guard has convinced us that work is the most important part of our universe when in actuality it is just the thing that we have to do to sustain the more important parts of our life, like our families, hobbies and homes. We are told that we must show up to work with brave faces and dry cheeks in the midst of heartbreak, sickness and chaos. That is not reality. Impactful leaders know that the human experience is messy and give grace to allow people to experience the mess. Those leaders know that it is impossible for each of our people to show up at their best everyday because we know we don't show up at our best every day.

The majority of people would not continue to do their job for free; they do it because capitalism requires it of us. If we were all offered the same money to not work, many of us would opt for not working. Personally, I'd rather be butt naked on a boat, yet I'm not. Work is something we do, it is not something we are, and we should be given the space to step away when the parts of our lives that take precedence are messy. When we talk about leadership that matters, we're not talking about the ability to measure KPIs, track metrics, and generate revenue; we are talking about your ability to make people feel seen, heard, and valued. The rest comes. People perform their best when they feel safe to be exactly who they are in that moment, in that day, in this life.

Safety isn't just some fun buzzword people made up to get into the algorithm; it's not just some "woke liberal agenda." Safety is a business practice. Admittedly, I hate the "business case" argument for initiatives like this because creating spaces where humans feel safe *should* be the bare minimum, but unfortunately, it's not. Creating safe work environments isn't just an HR problem or a better handbook problem. Sometimes, our companies are the only safe space our employees might have, and people deserve at least a portion of their day where they can take a deep breath and just exist.

We have to bake safety into our every day business practices. It's more than a Black History Month email or a Pride banner on Zoom; it is inherently creating an environment where people are given the tools to thrive.

Protecting Yourself When You Aren't Safe

I recognize that many of us don't get to choose who manages us and do not have the privilege of leaving. We don't all get to work with managers who want to build a better future, and I want to make sure you're seen here, too.

You deserve to feel safe at work. If you don't feel safe, please take the steps to guard your mental health, or in the words of professor, author, and advocate Elizabeth Leiba, "Protect Your Peace." No job is worth your mental health, your physical health, or your family. Do your job, but do not let it consume you. Do not let the fear, the angst, or the dread eat you alive.

Even if you do not have the space to leave your job or manager, there are some steps you can take to protect yourself:

- Document, document, document, not necesarily for them but for you. One day, someone will make you believe that it is all in your head; it's not.
- Talk to someone. There is no shame in therapy.
- Build community; it can be very grounding to surround yourself with people who have similar lived experiences.
- Don't doubt yourself; you are not less than because others do not see your value.
- Take your paid time off (PTO) if you have it. Your benefits are part of your compensation; utilize them.
- If you are looking for another job, build your network intentionally. Most job seekers are landing their next role through connections, not cold applies.

You Are the Answer

Whether you are a manager who is looking to become better or someone looking to confirm you deserve better, the world needs you. We move forward only by acknowledging what hasn't worked and being willing to intentionally do things differently, and it doesn't mean it's the right way the first time or even the tenth time. What matters is that the world deserves better and better comes from action. Safety comes from action. Creating a safer work space, a safer world, and a safe path forward cannot just be done in block paragraphs on our social media pages; we must be willing to do the hard work, and the hard work starts with you, standing in front of the mirror and meeting yourself for the first time.

5 | Broken

"Blessed are the cracked, for they let in the light."

—Spike Milligan

You Are Not Broken

You are not broken. You are not broken because you have caused harm. You are not broken because you have experienced harm. You are not broken because you experience the full spectrum of human emotion.

Do not let Instagram fool you; life is not painted in shades of beige, white, and eggshell.

You are not millennial beige; you are so much more.

It's easy to fall down the rabbit hole of the social media we are surrounded with. Every day, we are fed content that tells us how to heal, when to heal, and only when we have done those things are we deserving of love, of life, of whatever it is that they're selling. We are sold the idea that we are broken because it keeps us searching for the solve, the cure, the magic button that makes the human experience make sense.

69

I have bad news for you: The human experience is messy, and it doesn't get less messy with "self-care," fad diets, or even with therapy. We are never done healing, we are never done evolving, we are never done because the human experience is not linear. There isn't a "final boss" of life; there isn't a winner. The truth is sometimes we win, sometimes we lose, and most of the time we are simply winging it.

Don't Let Your Ego Get in Your Way

As humans, we are fed the narrative that you have two choices: you can be a good person, or you can be a bad person. There is no room for gray areas. We are sorted into binary categorizations and left to sort it out. The actuality of life is that we are simply people. All of us will do good things, bad things, beautiful things, hurtful things for our whole lives.

Nothing in this life is black and white and certainly not the way we experience the world. However, the belief that we are the worst (or best) thing we have ever done doesn't serve us; it holds us back.

Fundamentally, (most) people want to be good people. They want to be good neighbors, bosses, co-workers, partners, friends, and parents. The idea that our past behavior makes us a "bad person" will also keep us from examining it. Oftentimes, the hardest conversations we have with ourselves are the ones where we have to call ourselves in and acknowledge that we have caused harm.

Our ego does not want us to be a "bad person," so it slips into denial and moves into the defensive. How many times have we heard people explain away their harm with sentences like "I can't be racist; my cousin's husband's sister's landlord is [insert indentity]?"

We would rather let our egos convince us that we couldn't possibly have caused hurt because we are "good" rather than allowing the shame, guilt, and the knot in our throats to teach us how to do better the next time. We don't get to decide if we hurt someone else; if they are hurt, they are hurt. Our ego's flawed perception of our behavior doesn't change that fact.

The easiest thing we can do is say sorry, do the work to understand their hurt, and try to do better next time.

Don't let your ego stunt your journey, because if you let your ego lead you, it will take you on a detour. Your ego isn't your friend in the journey of trying to lead an authentic life because your ego will always run from your shadow. To truly find the most authentic version of yourself, you have to be willing to meet your shadow eye to eye and acknowledge the power it holds.

Your ego will always be the monster under your bed if you allow it. Oftentimes, we view our ego as vanity, how we view our image, our body, or what we own; however, your ego goes much deeper than that. Your ego cares how you are perceived, not only by yourself but by the world around you, and that also means your ego runs from your failures, your faults, and the things you feel shame around. Your ego will lie to you; your ego will be try to convince you that if you own up to the things you have done, then you must be undeserving of a life worth living. It will convince you that you do not deserve love, acceptance, or fullfillment. Your ego will feed you the lie that you are broken.

You are not a broken person for causing harm, but that doesn't mean you don't have to be willing to look it in the eye and acknowledge its existence. You are responsible for how you show up in this life, but just because you don't always get it right doesn't mean you have to punish yourself for an eternity.

I have good news and bad news, and it's the same news: You will get it wrong forever. That also means you get to keep trying, learning, and doing better, forever. You will get it wrong forever because even those who are actively healing cause harm.

It's just what humans do. Human interaction and communication are the hardest things we will ever do. They will always be complex and complicated, no matter how many TikToks you watch about five steps to not argue with your partner; you will still argue with your partner. What we learn is how to approach arguments in a better way.

Healing Is Hectic

Your healing never ends; don't believe Instagram. However, just because it doesn't end doesn't mean it doesn't get easier with time. You do not have to be perfect to be worthy of speaking kindly to yourself.

For a long time, I thought all of the people who were out living must have cracked the code to true healing. I believed that I deserved a good life, a soft life, an abundant life once I had atoned for all of the wrong I had perceived that I had done. I convinced myself that a life worth living was simply on the other side of healing. I did all of the therapy, I did all of the journaling, I did all of the things that I was supposed to do, and it still didn't feel like enough. How often do we convince ourselves that we'll start to live after we finish this "phase," after this next promotion, or when life gets less hectic?

No one tells you that healing is chaotic, it's ugly, and it's certainly not linear. One day, you're thriving, you haven't thought of the old versions of you in months, and a day later you're crumpled in a heap on the floor unable to catch your breath because you cannot get the thoughts to stop. That version of healing isn't as aesthetic as an "eat pray love" trip to Italy, so we see much less of it online, but that is much more common than pasta in Italy.

That version of ourselves can feel so shameful, so unworthy of care, that it's easy to feel pathetic—that version of you is the version that needs the most care, the most kindness, the most space to feel.

> The only way to heal is to let yourself experience your experiences.
> You can't workout your way into healing.
> You can't "treat yourself" your way into healing.
> You can't outwork your way into healing.
> You can't ignore your way into healing.
> You have to make intentional space for healing while also recognizing it is not a one-stop shop, and the process of healing never ends.

And even on your journey to healing, you will hurt others, and you will experience hurt and all of the other things. Life keeps life-ing, and you will constantly have to stop to remind yourself to breathe, feel, and experience.

> I won't lie to you, the process of healing is hectic.
> Life is hectic.
> The whole experience of being on Earth in the 2020s is hectic.

If I have learned anything, it seems life is simply getting more hectic.

Life continues to get more hectic, and work continues to get more hectic. The emails keep coming, and the meetings get longer and more frequent; it doesn't stop.

Leading with Humanity

Don't wait for life to get less messy to start treating yourself and those around you with humanity. As leaders, co-workers, and peers, too often we forget that the people on the side of the conference table or email are people too, going through the same yet different chaos.

We are quick to turn on our "HR, per my last email, cc their boss" voices without thinking about how we can approach hard conversations with care and the recognition that work is not the most important thing; *it is just the thing we are focused on in this moment.* Instead of trying to shame people into productivity, we should be thinking about how we can better support them to allow them the space to be more productive. Shame does not produce results; it simply produces shame, fear, and hidden experiences.

It is okay to ask our teams what they need from us, and we should be asking that, but it means we must be prepared for the answers that come with those questions. Human needs are complex, and sometimes we need more than a $10 Uber Eats gift card.

> You cannot solve global crisis with a pizza party.
> You cannot solve grief with a Band-Aid.
> Most likely you cannot solve anything; you can simply listen, support, and extend care where you can.

As a Type A, Virgo, only child, I am by nature a problem solver, and it has been hard for me to learn I cannot solve everything because not every problem has a solution. Emotions are one of those things. We cannot solve emotion; we can simply be willing to sit with them when they are our own emotions and be willing to listen when others need it.

Oftentimes, as leaders it is easy to keep our conversations curt, cold, and impersonal because it is much easier to look at data and facts rather than taking human emotions into account, which make it messy. That mess isn't as scary as you think because it is the single thing that connects all humans. The mess may look different, but it exists for all of us.

COVID-19 was a single moment in time where the entire world experienced a macro trauma collectively. We were navigating crisis, loss, fear, and the unknown together even without knowing one another. We experienced the turmoil that came with 2020. It didn't matter your title, your age, your salary, whom you loved, or where you lived—we lived that chaos together.

Chaos like that happens on the micro and macro level everyday. In 2020, I remember having a meltdown on my floor wondering how I was going to pretend to lead my team while also having the weight of George Floyd's murder sitting on my heart. How could we ask people to work through communal heartache like this?

Yet we do it every day. We expect people to come to work as if their personal lives come second to who they actually are. People experience divorce, illness, death, financial issues, trauma, and chaos regularly yet are forced to come to work and send their happy little emails and join their silly little meetings like their worlds are not crumbling around them. If they fail to do so, they fear they will be let go.

Work is not more important than our hearts, and I will die on that hill.

Rejecting Bad Leadership

Earlier in my career, I worked for a well-known tech company. It was the only company that I ever worked at where crying in the bathroom was a normal part of many of our lives. Even now, my previous co-workers and I joke about being trauma bonded from working there, and there is a lot of truth in that. When I was working there, there were many dehumanizing moments, but one that rings clearly in my memory.

It was the weekend after Valentine's Day, and my dog had suddenly gotten sick, so I had to make the unplanned decision to put him to sleep. Needless to say, I was hysterical. On Monday morning, I found myself still crumpled in the fetal position in my bed surrounded by tissues, sobbing.

There was no chance of me being a functional human who could go to work and not cry at my desk. I grabbed my laptop and penned an email to my boss, the CFO, and let him know what events had unfolded the previous day and told him I would need to take the day off.

His response? "You will need to be at the office today." That's it. No "I'm sorry." Just a simple order to resume my usual day of email sending. When I let him know I still would not be coming, he informed me that my "insubordination" would earn me a write-up.

He didn't see my grief as grief; he saw it as an annoyance.

He didn't see my loss as a loss but as an inconvenience to the business.

I never went back.

I want to recognize that being able to leave your job when they dehumanize you is a privilege, one many of us do not have. I am not saying to risk your livelihood because bad leaders exist, but I hope to help you recognize that bad leaders do not have to be normalized.

We may not all have the space to leave our jobs and start over, but we must take the steps and the space to manage and heal from our grief.

Grief is not linear, but here are some ways to acknowledge it:

Let yourself feel: You cannot run from grief, you can only prolong it, let yourself sit with the feelings.

Find rituals that ground you: Whether it's journaling, picking up heavy weights, or lighting a candle, find moments that ground you.

You're on your own time: There's no timeline for grief, and it is certainly not linear. It's okay if you don't feel better today, or even tomorrow; grief is a process with no set timetable.

Let love in: Grief can make you want to shut the world out, but let people in. Let them love you; let them hold you.

Don't hold it in: Let your feelings out, the grief, the rage, the confusion. Let it all out.

Listen to your body: Grief isn't just emotional; it's physical, too. Listen to what your body needs.

Honor what was, embrace what is: Find ways to honor the person, relationship, or situation you are grieving. It's okay to acknowledge how important it was to you; it is not less meaningful because it ended.

Give yourself permission to experience joy: It's okay to laugh, to find moments of peace, to live fully. Joy doesn't erase grief—they can coexist, and joy is an act of resistance.

To this day, he looks at my LinkedIn pretty regularly; I hope my whole existence gives him heartburn.

Bad leaders deserve to be recognized, and bad behavior deserves to be called out. Bad leaders have existed for so long because we were told there weren't other options.

There are other options.

Embracing Good Leadership

Good leaders exist because they choose to do the hard work and not just the easy work. Good leaders don't exist by chance; they choose to be human, to be authentic, and to show up in their truth.

Good leaders let life happen.

Good leaders ask people how they can support them.

Good leaders care about the people they're leading.

And sometimes that means facts and data take a backseat while we let people just let life happen.

When I say good leaders let life happen, I do not just mean to their teams; I mean to themselves as well. The most powerful thing we can do as a leader is to mirror the behavior we want to encourage. We also have to know when to stop to let life happen to us too.

We cannot pretend to be unbreakable and expect our teams to be willing to be vulnerable. We must be willing to be vulnerable first with ourselves and then with our teams.

We are taught that we must be resilient. As a Black woman, I am constantly fed content about how resilient we are and how we must continue to be strong. As a person, a partner, a peer, and a leader, I do not want to always be strong; sometimes, I want to soften my approach, my life, my day, and my conversations.

I want people to feel the same with me. I do not expect my teams to put on happy smiles just to meet with me. I don't expect them to give me made up BS answers to keep the conversation light. I do not place expectations on the emotions of others. All I want is for the people on my teams, in my orgs, and in my life to feel like they can put down their sword with me because it is safe here.

The Magic of Being Human

I aim to create spaces where people can feel safe to simply exist because there is magic in that.

There is magic in seeing the light in the cracks of not only ourselves but those around us. Our power is in our cracks, in our flaws, in our histories, in our stories. When we require our teams to shut out their truth, we shut out their magic, and we strip them of their power.

We curate the spaces that our teams experience at work, and those spaces can look like a battlefield or a safe haven; it is up to us as peers and leaders to determine what environment we create.

There is no benefit in leading with fear except for your ego, and we already know how far that gets us.

People perform better when they feel safe to be exactly who they are and exactly who they are comes with baggage (even if you choose to ignore that fact). No one is capable of being at 100% every day, in life, at work, at home. Some days, we are just not on our A game, and that is okay.

We are humans, not performers. All we can ask of people is to be human.

For so much of our careers, we are taught that our emotions are a roadblock, a hindrance, and an annoyance to those around us—that is a lie that only serves capitalism.

Do not skip your grief to keep your boss happy.
Do not skip your happy to keep your boss happy.
Do not skip your needs to keep your boss happy.

You are the sum of all of your parts, and that is where your magic lies: in the mess, in the grit, in the absolute truth of your experiences. You do yourself a disservice by making your emotions palatable so that your organization will find you to be acceptable.

I am not saying to go to work and scream and throw stuff off of your desk although I recognize the desire: I am saying do not let yourself suffer alone internally for eight hours a day to make someone else money. Pretending your emotions don't exist can be a lonely place. Putting on a happy and brave face often only amplifies the feelings inside of you.

You deserve your feelings, and you deserve to own them as you experience them, not when it is convenient for the rest of the world. You are not broken because you feel things. Feeling things is simply how you know you are alive.

6 | Apologies in the Mirror

Your Experiences Don't Dictate Your Value

You are not the worst thing that's ever happened to you, but it's easy to believe that you are. So much of who we are is dictated by what happens to us. Our experiences shape our identities, our futures, and how we show up in the world. Our brains often use our worst experiences to determine our worth. Your worth has nothing to do with how others treat you. Your value is inherent; it exists regardless of what you experience.

They often say that a break is better than a fracture. Fractures never heal right. We think they're healed, and then all of a sudden, you're sitting with ice on your ankles. It seems as if each time someone undervalues us, it rips a piece off, and each time we become smaller and smaller until there is nothing left. This is true regardless of whether it is an abusive partner, a toxic friendship, domineering parents, a demeaning boss, a childhood bully, a random act of violence, or the accumulated microaggressions of society.

This experience transcends our personal relationships and floods into all parts of our lives. We seek acceptance from our families, from our friends, from our partners, from our communities, and from our jobs. Humans are communal, and it makes sense that we crave acceptance so deeply, but it doesn't mean it isn't a harmful way to frame our self-worth.

Capitalism vs. Humanity

Our jobs often become tied in with our identities, and our professional experiences impact us more than we are willing to recognize. We are taught to believe that trauma is a normal side effect from work, the barter we make in exchange for a paycheck.

Work shouldn't be a source of trauma, yet for so many of us, it is. For so many of us, it is the thing that we think will break us. We trust our employers want the best for us, but so many of us have stories that contradict that idea.

In 2020, we witnessed an influx of organizations publicly declaring their commitment to change, to take responsibility for the harm they had caused, and to transform their ways. Many organizations made bold promises, claiming they were ready to do the hard work to create equitable safe environments. Yet, as the months passed, it became painfully obvious that so many of these "promises" were rooted in PR and marketing, not in humanity. Rather than following through on tangible action, they were rooted in Instagram posts, marketing campaigns, and lies. These organizations paid lip service to the issues at hand without every addressing the root causes.

After the tragic murder of George Floyd, the world was shaken, and businesses scrambled to make public statements. The year 2020 was filled with events that required public statements, from COVID to George Floyd to Breonna Taylor to the fight against stopping Asian American hate. For each event, companies quickly put out messages solidifying their support with each community, vowing to fight for safety, and vowing to try to change the world. There was PR statement after PR statement, yet no one stopped to listen to these communities. They exacerbated every issue they claimed to address. In the end, rather than healing the wounds, they dug their bare hands into the wound and ripped it further apart. Empty promises only deeped the mistrust, disappointment, and general disdain for corporate spaces, leaving those who truly worked to make change feeling exhausted, unheard, and unsupported.

Since 2020, we have seen organizations make empty pledges to protect their humans, to value their safety, and to put people above profits. It sounded too good to be true, because it was. Capitalism wins every time, and capitalism has never cared about the safety, mental health, or well-being of its constituents.

It felt defeating, to see the bright light of potential progress only to have it snuffed out as quickly as it was lit. I spent a lot of time thinking about what I could have done differently to deserve different experiences from my companies or different outcomes with those I have spent time educating, and unfortunately, the answer is, there is nothing any of us could have done.

In a world dictated by capitalism, which we are forced to participate in, humanity rarely wins.

Blame and Forgiveness

People will mistreat you forever unfortunately. We are not in control of how other people treat us, but we are responsible for how we respond, how we move forward, and how we heal.

In our careers, we will inevitably experience many kinds of people, and some of those people will be people we talk about in therapy. We will have bosses, colleagues, and peers who are unkind to us, and we will inevitably spend a lot of time trying to figure out the "why." Human nature loves to ask "why." We love to be able to wrap things up in neat little packages. However, the "why" isn't always that easy.

It is easy to blame ourselves for the way people treat us because it is often easier to take responsibility than to try to figure people out. We love to blame ourselves, karma, their star sign, but the truth of the matter is, some people aren't kind, some people aren't nice, and some people will treat you poorly regardless of how you treat them.

You are not defined by how others treat you. In this life, we will all do many good things, and we will also do some not so great things. We often use those "not so great things" to tell ourselves that we deserve our trauma.

And just as you are not the worst thing that has ever happened to you, you are also not the worst thing you have ever done. Forgive yourself for the versions of you that didn't know any better. Our journey through this messy life should be filled with learning, growth, and movement forward; it is okay that you are no longer the person you used to be.

When I left a particularly abusive relationship, I carried a lot of internalized self-hatred, anti-Blackness, and general discontent. I was hurt, I was scared, and I was unsure of myself. The world had shown me that I couldn't trust anyone but myself, and I walked back into the world guarded. When I finally began dating again, I met a man who was an unexpected gift, a gift I didn't recognize until many years later.

Throughout our relationship, I was an unhealed nightmare. I was closed off, I was mean, I was inconsiderate, and I didn't care. I sought out conflict because it was what I was used to, and in that, I said things that I now deeply regret. He was always kind and gentle with me, and I still refused to trust it. I broke his heart.

Two weeks before a planned cross-country move together, I sent the text, "We should just break up." It was out of the blue at least for him. I was annoyed that he had eaten my leftovers, and this seemed like a valid response. As soon as I sent the text, I broke down into hysterics because even I couldn't understand why I would intentionally ruin something so good.

It was because I didn't believe I deserved it. The unhealed version of me was insistent on staying in pain, in continuing the cycle I had lived in for so long because the unhealed version of me was convinced I didn't deserve better.

It has been many, many, many years since that story, and when I think about the person I was then, I am not proud. I am immediately met with the stomach-turning feeling of shame. I can feel the guilt, the sadness, and the confusion rushing back to me.

What I have learned is not to run from that shame but to look at it head-on. It has taken me years to stop burying that version of myself, pretending it didn't exist and instead to forgive her. You must be willing to forgive yourself over and over again. Although I am not proud of the person I was back then, I do recognize that she was doing what she could with the tools she had in her toolbox at the time. She is the version that kept me alive.

Forgive yourself, too. You will have many moments where the future versions of you will cringe, will feel shame, and will feel hurt. Forgive every version of yourself because each version of you will have a different set of tools and capabilities. As you continue to grow, develop, and elevate, you will begin to recognize when you've caused harm, and although it is uncomfortable, it is growth. Do not begin to resent your past self, but instead release that version with love and forgiveness.

Healing doesn't mean you forget what has happened to you or the harm you have caused. Healing makes you more aware of yourself, your feelings, and your needs, but it doesn't erase the past; it simply allows you to move forward. Healing isn't easy, and it often doesn't feel good. Healing can manifest in many ways, but it certainly isn't linear. Healing isn't a yoga class or a week of PTO. Healing requires intentional work, healing often requires therapy, and healing requires being willing to feel your feelings rather than doomscrolling your way through them.

Scrolling for Dopamine

The Internet has offered many of us an escape from ourselves. So many of us replace healing with wellness accounts, instant dopamine hits, and impulse buying. I am guilty of it, too. I am an active member of the "treat culture club." Bad day? Treat. Good day? Treat. Stressed? Treat. I realized that I was coping with hard feelings through searching for dopamine online.

The instant gratification of treats and the Internet cannot replace actual healing. Practice asking yourself, "Am I doing this because I want to, or am I doing this to avoid feeling an uncomfortable feeling right now?"

You are not alone in trying to dopamine your way out of uncomfortable feelings. It has been normalized and pushed on us since the dawn of the Internet. Companies like Amazon prey on your desire for dopamine hits and use science-backed methodology to ensure we continue to click "buy now."

How do we break the cycle of running from our feelings? That piece is harder than buying the new sweater or the $8 coffee. The only way to get out is through. It is a cliché but one that holds merit.

Don't Run Away from Yourself

So many of us are simply running from ourselves. We are running from ourselves, from our shame, from our past, and from our bullies, and we choose to run full speed at all of the things that will make us forget instead of running toward the things that make us remember.

I am not saying we should dwell on the things that make us feel sadness, shame, or heartache, but we must acknowledge that they exist. We can heal from our experiences only if we are willing to actually experience them. So many of us numb our feelings with social media, alcohol, or drugs instead of reaching into our core and solving for the root problem.

Do not dwell in your heartache, but let yourself feel it; let yourself experience it. We can heal only from that which we truly understand. Do not run from yourself instead, find a way home to yourself. You are your home, and the longer you run from you, the longer your trauma will linger, and the longer it will pull you back into it depths.

Healing Is a Process

Healing isn't linear, and it certainly isn't easy. Don't expect for healing to take a day, a week, or even a month. Healing is an onging process and one that is full of setbacks, surprises, and uncomfortable moments. Sit with yourself in the uncomfortable silence, sit with yourself in the moments that feel like you want to disappear, and, more importantly, love yourself in the moments that make you feel unlovable.

Journal, write it down, get it out. You do not have to lock it all inside. It is real whether you keep it inside or not. Your life does not have to be a secret locked away deep inside your chest. Your life is not something to feel shame around but something to be lived out loud and wholly.

You are whole even with all of your mess.
You are whole even with all of your mistakes.
You are whole even with all of your hurt.

We are not broken; we are simply experience the messiness that life has given us. The good news is that everyone has mess. The bad news is everyone has mess. Do not let the mess of others dictate your worth, and heal your mess so you do not project it onto others. We will all do good things and bad things for the rest of our lives. There will never be a time when we get it completely right; we will always have space to do better. Do not let your ego keep you from continuously searching for growth, do not let it keep you from apologizing, and do not let it keep you from examining your own life.

Self-examination is a gift, one so many of us leave unopened. The ability to learn from where you have been is a gift. Do not feel shame for the things you have done and experienced, but thank those times for having allowed you to grow into the person you are today and will continue to become.

You can say goodbye to that person, but you can do it with love and gratitude for all they were willing to teach you.

7

Standing on Business

"You were not just born to center your entire existence on work and labor. You were born to heal, to grow, to be of service to yourself and community, to practice, to experiment, to create, to have space, to dream, and to connect."
—Tricia Hersey, *Rest Is Resistance: A Manifesto*

Burnout by Design

Do you even know who you are anymore? I'm not trying to throw some spiritual curveball here, but let's be honest. In the grind of life, it's way too easy to forget to check in with yourself. We're constantly running around making sure everyone else is fed, watered, and taken care of. We cook. We clean. We go to work. We go through the motions until we've built ourselves into robots doing what's expected of us.

- Go to work
- Pick up the kids
- Make dinner

- Feed the dog
- Do the laundry
- Try to work out
- Wash, rinse, repeat

Our lives become a revolving checklist.

We only have 24 hours in each day, and ideally eight of those are spent sleeping. If the other eight are spent working, we are left with eight hours that we own, but do we really own them when we have to also manage our households, attempt to take care of our bodies, and find time to relax?

Whoever said me and Beyoncé have the same 24 hours in a day lied.

And somewhere among working overtime, checking emails in bed, and showing up to events just because we have to, we lose ourselves. We get caught in the grind, telling ourselves it's "temporary," that "we're just hustling for a little while," or that we'll "catch up on rest next week." But week after week, month after month, we keep running the same cycle, convincing ourselves this is normal. This is what success looks like.

But somewhere in the process, we forget to ask ourselves what we actually need and what we actually want. We neglect our health, our relationships, our passions, and even our sense of self. We convince ourselves that as long as we keep moving and as long as we keep hitting those goals and making progress, everything will be fine. But the truth is losing yourself at the expense of yourself is not "fine," and it's certainly not worth it. And no matter how many spa days or summer Fridays you plan, your body will catch up with you. Your energy will run dry. Your creativity will fizzle out. And when it does, you'll realize that the thing you've been chasing all along—the next promotion, the bigger paycheck, the dream job—wasn't ever going to be enough.

You know what is enough? You. Your health, your boundaries, your well-being, and the space to rest and reset.

Burnout doesn't happen overnight; it's a slow burn, and it's one that can sneak up on you if you're too lost in hustle culture. The Maslach Burnout Inventory, which is one of the most recognized tools for measuring burnout, suggests that around 77% of workers experience symptoms of burnout at some point in their careers. Almost everyone you meet will have a run in with burnout at least once in their career. Capitalism will run us into the ground if we let it.

Burnout is easier to prevent than it is to cure. Burnout is a deep rooted symptom of capitalism, and we are told to chalk it up to being "workaholics" or "boss babes," but what we are really doing is ignoring the needs of our bodies for the sake of systems that have no stake in our well-being. We are taught from a very young age that our ability to earn an income is the most important part of the universe; in turn, we relate our own value to the titles we hold.

Why are we willing to sacrifice our families, our hobbies, and our youth for a system that doesn't care if we live or die? It's a never-ending corporate ladder filled with goal posts that always move. You think "If I just work hard until I make [x] salary, I'll take a break" or "Once I get that title, I'll take my partner on vacation" or "Once I get into [x] company, I'll start focusing on my kids/family"—but capitalism is a lie, and we are never satisfied. We always want more. We get the salary and start thinking about how we can make more money. We get the title, and we're already looking on how to move further. We get into the dream company, and now we're trying to figure out how to climb that ladder. Capitalism works as it is intended to; our burnout is by design.

Creating Tomorrow's Memories Today

I am a notorious "work from PTO, PTOer," as many of us are. It feels like truly stepping away from our careers can be detrimental to our careers. This thought is always at the back of my mind:

"What if they realize they don't need me?"

I hate to be the bearer of bad news, but something we should all know about capitalism is that it has never needed us and we are all replaceable. You know who doesn't think you're replaceable? Your dog. Your family. The people who love you—but definitely your dog.

Recently, for the first time in my entire career, I went away and left my laptop at home. I got to step away, uninterrupted, and focus on the people, the places, the activities that I love without the Google chat sound in the background. I was present with my family, and I was actively involved in the things we were doing. I got to connect with the people I love without the nagging dread of my email inbox.

This break wasn't a long one, but it was enough time for me to realize that the center of my universe is not work. Work is the thing that simply sustains the things that are the center of my universe. My family, my partner, my pets, my hobbies are things that make life worth living, not work. I realized that I don't melt if I set boundaries and step away.

Life is short. You don't have forever. These moments, these jobs, the people you love—one day all you will have is your memories, and you are in control of how those memories are shaped. Are they filled with vacations where you are disconnected? Are they filled with missed soccer games and anniversaries? Or are they filled with the faces, emotions, and voices of the people you love?

It is incredibly easy to take time, life, and moments for granted when you believe that moments are infinite. Over the last few months, I've spent a lot of time thinking about mortality and what that means. It also means I've spent a lot of time thinking about what moments are most important to me and what moments I am most proud of.

What moments are most important to you? What moments are you most proud of? When you think back to your Rolodex of favorite memories, how many of them include work emails you've sent or decks you've presented? Probably not many.

I've also sat and thought about the concept of regret. I've never regretted spending time with the people I love, but I have regretted not being present because I was too absorbed with work.

Earlier in my career, when I had earned my first executive role, I remember it was a busy day a few days before Christmas. Everything was on fire, from customer issues to employee issues. My Slack inbox was dinging so constantly it sounded like a Spotify playlist. The same day, my dog was lethargic, not interested in eating. I wasn't incredibly worried; she was just a baby, a year old. My partner was off and brought the dog to the vet since I was unable to step away.

It had been a few hours, and when my phone rang, I thought nothing of it. Yet my partner's voice broke on the other end of the phone and told me there was nothing the vets could do, and they were going to have to put our dog to sleep. I was hysterical and still flipping between Slack messages and Shopify tabs.

I didn't step away. I couldn't; I didn't know how. I let my partner deal with the weight of putting our dog to sleep, and I stole my own final goodbye with her. When I think about regret, I think about this moment often. It is one of the moments that I find hard to forgive myself for. I allowed my job to steal a moment from me that I will never get back.

So, this is your reminder that if our only moments are work, if our only memories are work, we will have missed out on life. It is easy to get wrapped up in hustle culture. Capitalism is blinding. It is easy to believe you're different, your job is different, you are different. You aren't. None of us can out-hustle capitalism; it will run you over every time.

It is easy to get lost in the sea of just wanting to get one step further, only to find out that one step never feels like it's enough. Capitalism will be a death sentence if you let it: to your home, to your body, to your mind. It takes without guilt; it steals without apology. Do not let it steal the moments you want to have, the moments that you will look back on with regret if you miss them. You'll probably never regret spending time with the people you love, but you'll definitely regret not being present because you were too absorbed with work.

You Are More Than Your Work

Work is work. Work is not your family. Work is not you. You are more than your work, your title, and your income. Your value doesn't lie in what you are willing to sacrifice for your job. Your value doesn't lie in your title or income. Your value is not tied to your ability to be the most disconnected.

Work is just work, but you? You are so much more than work. You are loved. You are valued. You are deserving of rest. You are deserving of a soft life. You are deserving of time for the things and people you love. You are deserving of a life full of uninterrupted experiences.

Take time to make memories with the people who love you. Take time to be present with the people who see you. Take time to honor that one day memories will be all we have left.

You have to be willing to set boundaries with capitalism and stand on them. It is easy to bend your boundaries for what feels like growth, but those bends will lead to burnout, and that burnout will lead to chaos.

One of the hardest things you will do as a human is to learn about yourself and your needs and then set the boundaries required to protect your peace. It is easy to neglect your own needs when you constantly tell yourself "I'm good."

Are you good? Are you actually healing, or are you just filling your life with distractions to keep you from thinking about what is hurting you? When was the last time you asked yourself how you were doing and gave yourself an honest answer? When was the last time you asked yourself what you needed and then provided yourself with those things?

When was the last time you asked yourself how your heart was and stayed silent enough to actually hear the answer?

Being Vulnerable Instead of Being a Martyr

We hear a lot of talk about vulnerability in the workplace, especially as leaders, but we forget to mention that to be vulnerable with others, we must first be willing to be vulnerable with ourselves. Being vulnerable with ourselves is not easy. I would rather tell a stranger my deepest secrets than to unpack them in the mirror; yet we don't realize that so often we are the stranger. We spend so much time curating the perfect persona, yet we have become complete strangers to ourselves.

Being vulnerable with yourself is not for the weak, it is not easy, and it takes hard work. You must be willing to crack yourself open and look inside your chest and touch the parts that hurt. It requires you to look that hurt in the eyes and invite it to sit with you. It means looking at your mistakes, your regrets, and the hurt you have caused, and accept it.

Sometimes, we lose our spark; I know I do. Sometimes, I feel uncreative, and I feel as if I cannot words together, pick up a pen to write, or even film content. I find myself getting frustrated at the smallest mistakes and getting angry at the easiest tasks. When this happens, it forces me to ask myself, "What isn't working?" When was the last time you asked yourself what isn't working and what is draining you?

When we ask ourselves complex questions, we are often met with complex answers. We can be met with answers we weren't ready for, goodbyes that rip our heart out, or habits we may not be ready to part with yet. Setting boundaries isn't just about not looking at your phone before bed or limiting your screen time. Setting boundaries will mean you have to part ways with people, things, and habits. When you begin to examine what isn't working, it forces you to examine what you're settling for and what topics you're dancing around instead of acknowledging who you are allowing to steal your spark. We avoid so much of this to avoid confrontation and instead end up in turmoil with ourselves.

We stay quiet, stay calm, and stay neutral about the things that we know eat away at us. We think it is the sacrifice we must make to preserve our jobs, marriages, and families. It is not your job to be the martyr, it is not your job to be the doormat, and you do not have to lay down and take it. Set your boundaries and stand on business.

When to Let Go OR What to Let of

Self-care is a loaded phrase these days; it has become the hottest trend on platforms like TikTok, and when we see videos go viral, they often look like spa days and retail therapy. People are still mistaking distraction for healing. Now, I am the first to say, I love a good massage and a new outfit, but that will not heal me; it will simply be a Band-Aid for the larger issue.

True self-care looks like tapping in with yourself to truly understand what your heart, mind, and body need and prioritizing yourself. Your body knows the relationships, places, jobs, and people who aren't right for you. Your body tells you: listen to it. Yet, we continue to ignore the signs our bodies give us to preserve the peace when sometimes you need to burn the bridge.

Self-care isn't just about preserving the things and people who are good for you; it is about clearing out the people and places that no longer serve you. To make room for better experiences, we must be willing to let go of the old ones. You must get comfortable with the notion that not all jobs, relationships, or experiences are meant to last forever; it doesn't make them less important or a wasted part of your story, but it means they cannot accompany you on the next part of your journey. Some things end, and that is okay.

I will not sugarcoat it and say that it's fun or all sunshine and rainbows. Goodbyes often feel bad even from jobs we knew were draining us or from friends who have never appreciated us.

As leaders, we know that goodbyes are hard, uncomfortable, and often tear filled. We feel guilty about leaving our teams in the hands of irresponsible companies. We feel guilty when we have to terminate people. We feel guilty when people leave because you couldn't protect them from a toxic work culture. Sometimes, self-care includes knowing what to let go.

Embracing Change So You Can Grow

Setting your boundaries will often look like change, and we know change is hard. However, your fear of change is what is holding you back in your journey to vulnerable leadership. Vulnerability starts with you, and often it requires change, not only to your environment but also to your habits. Growth requires change, and if you shy away from change, you shy away from growth. Sometimes, we avoid change to keep the people around us from having to meet the new versions of ourselves. The right people will embrace all versions of you with open arms.

Over your lifetime, you will meet many versions of yourself, and all of these versions were forged from your experiences, your needs, and your willingness to grow. Meet each version of yourself with acceptance, excitement, and the willingness to get to know them deeply. Every question you ask yourself today, you must ask all versions of yourself, forever.

We must be willing to break down our own walls not only for our sake but for the people around us. We are responsible for our own healing. As friends, partners, and leaders, our relationship with ourselves impacts every other relationship we have, and it impacts how we show up to work and to the world.

You cannot be the best leader for your teams if you are unwilling to be the best version of yourself, for yourself. You are your responsibility. Your wellness is your responsibility. Your life is your responsibility; take control of it.

It may seem less stressful to "leave it up to the universe," but that is not reality. Don't let the viral tarot readings on the Internet fool you; you own your life. First, you have to be willing to acknowledge that you are responsible for your reality, and then you must be willing to confront the demons that exist within it. None of us is free from hurt, from vices, or from the cold reality that the world can be a scary place, and that is okay. However, we are in control of how we react and how we address the situations we are faced with.

Leading with Vulnerability, Not Fear

As a leader, you must be willing to open with yourself about your needs and lived experiences because when you lock your emotions down and put your heart on "airplane mode," you lead through harshness, rather than humanity. Your strength is not in your rigidity but in your ability to lead softly.

It is easy to auto-default as a leader to a power and fear-based management style because we have not healed our own trauma and have been unwilling to set parameters with the things and people who harm us.

Harm is cyclical. When we lead with our own harm, we simply create more harmed team members and, inevitably, more harmed leaders. The inability to set boundaries in order to heal will be reflected in the experiences of our teams, often sending them into fight-or-flight mode and leaving them unwilling to be vulnerable with us in return.

The best teams do not thrive in fear but in the assuredness that they are safe to experience life as it happens and to feel safe in who they are with their organizations and their leadership.

Rest Is a Right

I get it, life keeps happening, hurt keeps happening, and it can feel like the thing burning you out is the world around you. It is okay to take a breath, take a moment, and step away. One of the most important boundaries you will learn to set is understanding when you are out of spoons and need to put it all down.

You cannot carry the weight of the world forever and expect not to crumble; you are simply one person with two hands. You cannot do it all, and you shouldn't have to. Life doesn't stop, regardless of your age, title, or position, so sometimes. You need to hit the "pause" button and spend some time alone with yourself.

Work will be here when you get back, so take the time, take the PTO, turn off the phone. Your teams need you to be human, and that means acknowledging that you are not a superhero and you need rest. Rest is your right; it is not an earned act or a reward. It is yours to have.

Identifying Your Boundaries

Boundaries are hard to conceptualize and even harder to hold yourself to, especially when it comes to work. It feels like work can sometimes be the only place where our boundaries don't matter. But they do.

Boundaries at work can look like:

- "I do not answer emails once I am home with my family on nights/weekends."
- "On Tuesday mornings, I go to Pilates, so I cannot begin my day earlier than 8 a.m."
- "It is important to me to attend my child's soccer games, so I have to leave by 5 p.m. every Thursday."
- "If we cannot engage in respectful conversations, let's reconnect once we have both had space to cool off."
- "I am not comfortable discussing this at work."
- "I am not able to take on additional unpaid responsibilities at this time, Employee Resource Groups (ERGs), Pride, etc."

For those who are looking for a new role, I recommend discussing your work boundaries in your interview. It is your interview as well, and it is important to talk about the things you need in order to thrive in your workplace. I often recommend that before beginning your job search, you create guidelines for yourself on what you need, what you cannot tolerate, and what is a "nice to have."

I have included an example here:

Need to Have	Cannot Have	Nice to Have
• An organization that prioritizes mental well-being	• A company that has not done the work to educate itself about inclusion and authenticity	• Guacamole in the kitchen
• Benefits that include marginalized families	• Leadership who yells or is disrespectful in times of tension	• Unlimited PTO
• Inclusive workplace that protects employees through intentional organizational design	• A company that cares about its people only in a good economy	• ClassPass or a gym membership
• Ability to work out before/after work without interruption	• Racism, homophobia, transphobia, xenophobia	• A remote office budget
• Generous PTO policy with the ability to actually disconnect during PTO	• A company that doesn't prioritize work/life balance and stepping away	• Continued education

This table can look however you need it to, but I create this table for all parts of my life from family interactions, friendships, relationships, and certainly work. If you are currently employed and not looking for a new role, it doesn't mean you can't make this table; you still should!

When you do this exercise, do it with your current job in mind and think about how you could better prioritize yourself and voice your needs in your workplace. Are you beginning to feel burned out? Spend some time thinking about what parts of your work have led you to that place.

For those who are in a work environment that will not allow them to set boundaries, use this exercise to evaluate what you want next, but also use it to evaluate where you can relieve other stressors in your life outside of work.

I recognize that being able to set boundaries at work is a privilege, but for it to be the norm, we must be willing to dismantle the systems that do not work. We must be willing to have these conversations out loud, and as leaders, we must be willing to lead by example.

Honor humanity by being human yourself, and all humans have boundaries.

Setting boundaries at work is one of the hardest things you'll ever do, especially when you're used to running on overdrive. It feels taboo to tell your job what you need from it instead of the other way around. Here's the truth—if you don't set boundaries, your job will step into your life and put its grubby hands on everything you love; it will take and take until there is nothing left but you and your unread emails.

So, how do you start setting boundaries at work without feeling like you're risking it all or being perceived as "difficult"?

Here's the thing: *your boundaries are not up for debate.* They're non-negotiable. I'm going to need you to practice saying that in the mirror several times to build your confidence.

First, you have to recognize that setting boundaries isn't about being rigid or defensive. It's about protecting your space, your peace, and your ability to show up as your best self—at work and outside of it.

1. **Figure out what you need.**

   Before you can even communicate your boundaries, you need to know what they are. Ask yourself: *When do I do my best work? How do I do my best work? What leaves me feeling anxious?* Maybe it's working past 6 p.m. every night. Maybe it's people expecting you to answer emails during your lunch break. Maybe it's being expected to make everyone's urgency your urgency. Whatever it is you need, you must name it, repeat it, and write it down.

2. **Communicate your boundaries with confidence.**

   Once you know your boundaries, you have to communicate them. You cannot expect people to know what they don't know. You do not have to be mean or abrupt, but you can be direct in how you communicate them. This means allowing yourself to say no when you are asked to work on a project that extends yourself too far or saying no when asked if you are able to stay late.

3. **Ditch the guilt.**

   It's normal to feel guilty. You might feel like you're letting your team or your manager down. But let me clear the air: *Your worth is not tied to your productivity.* Your value is inherent, regardless. If people make you feel bad about setting a boundary, they benefited from you having none and that's a red flag. Set the boundary anyway.

4. **Well-being > productivity.**

   I get it. We've been conditioned to believe we matter only when we're productive. But your health, your happiness, and your well-being are more important than that unread email. If you need to step away from your desk for an hour to recharge, *do it*. If you need a mental health day, *take it*. Booking a trip with your bestie? *Catch the flight*. Rest is also productive. You do not do anyone any favors by running yourself into the ground. You will actually be better equipped to handle your role when you also take care of yourself.

5. **Stand on business.**

Boundaries aren't a one-time thing, and you will have to most likely communicate them over and over again. Do not falter when the conversation becomes uncomfortable; that is when you need to lean in to your boundaries even more. Being consistent in your boundaries will teach people how to treat you.

6. **Say "no" without guilt.**

Saying "no" is an art form and not an easy one to become an expert in. Saying no is not a weakness but a strength. Recognizing when you cannot do more than you are already doing is a gift. And honestly, we could all benefit by saying no a little more often. Often, saying no can be an act of self-preservation, and in a world where work can run you over, it might be the most powerful tool in your toolbox.

7. **Your boundaries = your self-worth.**

Setting boundaries is a love letter to yourself. It is an act of self-service to show yourself how much you care for you; it is self-preservation. When you choose to respect your needs and communicate them, it lets the rest of the world follow suit. Protecting your space is an act of courage.

It's not easy. It's not quick. But it's necessary. Understanding your boundaries is a lifelong journey. The longer you practice your boundaries, the better you will get at holding the line.

So, get clear on what you need, communicate those boundaries unapologetically, and protect your peace. You're not just saving yourself from burnout instead, you're setting the example for your teams to do the same. If we had the space to start setting boundaries, we can begin to reimagine what work could look like. And who doesn't want a world where work sucks less?

So, what are your boundaries? What will you do to protect them today? Write them down, and repeat them to yourself. Even if you don't have the courage to enforce them yet, let's get clear on what they are.

I've said it before, but it's worth mentioning again, burnout is easier to prevent than it is to cure, so it benefits us to begin to understand the things that are causing it so we can figure out how to step back and reevaluate.

Protecting Your Boundaries

A few years ago, during the great flight debacle of 2021, I had a heated encounter at the airline ticketing counter. I had an employee put her finger in my face when I showed her the flight I was trying to switch to on my phone. After she put her finger in my face, I asked her to please not do that. She proceeded to tell me that I was angry and offended "like the rest of my generation."

When I informed her that I was not angry, that I was speaking in my normal tone, and that I just don't tolerate or appreciate having a stranger's finger in my face, she told me, "We will have to agree to disagree, and you are what is wrong with the world." She deleted my seat from my flight before telling me she would not help me and walked away.

As a Black woman, I am all too aware that my boundaries can feel like an attack to those who never intended to respect or acknowledge my humanity. There are people who will never honor your boundaries regardless of how long you've known them or how clear you are about them.

Delete their seat in your life. The people who are unwilling to see your humanity, to see your healing, and to hear your needs are not your people.

You don't get to "agree to disagree" on emotions that do not belong to you.

Do not let other people make you feel as if your boundaries are dramatic or unnecessary. You are the curator of your space; protect it at all costs.

You are not a bad person for needing to set boundaries, and you are not mean for standing on them. The next time people try to overstep your boundaries and then shame you for it, ask them:

> *"Am I mean, or did I just not allow you to disregard my boundaries?"*

People will try to make you feel bad for protecting your peace and your wellness. Do not let them make you feel shame for doing the things you need to do to preserve yourself. Boundaries are self-preservation, and you are your own keeper. No one can protect you better than you can because only you can know what you need.

Do not shy away from grounding yourself in your needs. Do not run from the boundaries you require to be healthy. You deserve a life that feels good, at work and at play. Work doesn't have to suck, and it doesn't have to suck the life out of you.

May we be on a mission to make work suck less for ourselves and our teams. We are the future of work, and we get to decide what work will look like for the generations after us.

Will you decide to stand on business?

8

Let Them Lose You

Let Them

Life becomes easier when you learn that you cannot control the people around you. I have adopted the "let them" philosophy. I am going to let people act however they need to, and I will respond accordingly. You cannot decide how people show up, but you can decide how you want to be. You cannot decide how they treat you, but you can decide how you respond. You cannot decide if people choose to heal, but you can decide how you protect your peace. You cannot determine how people will react to the rawest version of yourself, but you can still choose to show up how you need to.

In work, in partnership, in family, and in life, humans seek to control the outcomes of their interactions. But the reality is that the only thing you are ever in control of is yourself—nothing more, nothing less. Control the controllable, which is not the people around you.

However, you can choose whom you allow around you and in your space.

It is so easy to take people's actions personally, but you're better off when you don't. How people treat us does not determine our value in the world. How people treat us does not reflect who we are. Instead, how people treat us is a mirror into how they feel about themselves. How people treat us is not up to us, but we get to choose how to move forward.

People will mistreat you, and it is not your fault. Let them, and then do what you need to do.

The hardest truth about finding your voice and walking in your own light is that it will always come with goodbyes. When you step into the best, messiest, realest version of yourself, many people will wonder what happened to the version of you that they concocted in their brain. For many of us, people pleasing is linked to the desire for acceptance and community. We want to be liked, we want to feel welcomed, and we want to be loved, but at what cost?

The authentic version of you will scare people away; let them lose you. Not everyone in our lives is meant to stay for the duration, and that is okay. The right people will gravitate toward you, while the wrong people inevitably see themselves out—if we let them. I personally have a bad habit of trying to hold onto people when I know that I need to let them go.

Learning to Let Go

I want to share my personal experience, which I hope can be a lesson in letting go that can help you.

In the summer of 2022, I was in a relationship with two partners, traveling the world and living my dream, at least that is what it looked like to the outside world. I put on my "happiest girl in the world" face for every photo, every piece of content I wrote, for every moment—just so that I wouldn't stir the pot. On the inside, I was unhappy, unsatisfied and wholly disinterested in this life

I had curated because it wasn't mine; it was someone else's. I had built this life for the consumption of others, not myself.

Life becomes hard when you stay in situations that do not fill your cup.

It is hard to be motivated when you spend a great deal of time faking being happy. Relationships, friendships, and situations end, yet oftentimes we hold on to them out of the desire for comfort, out of the desire to not cause hurt, and out of the desire to not have to explain.

I have a tendency to stay longer than I want or should because I hate hurting people, but staying doesn't avoid the hurt; instead, it prolongs it. Holding on to people out of fear is not a courageous act but a selfish one. This is a lesson I've learned and hope to hold onto although I am guilty of holding on for too long because just like you I'm just a human.

As humans, we will hurt the people we love, and hurt is unavoidable. How we reconcile with it is what matters.

Endings do not have to be cruel. Instead, endings should mirror the compassion we had in the beginning.

You do not do the people in your life a favor by staying when you want to go. You do not do yourself a favor by holding on to history. Staying in your comfort zone serves complacency, not your happiness.

Letting go does not mean your time was wasted but simply that your time together as partners, friends, or peers has come to an end.

Letting go is just one more season of life, and this season is about happiness. Chase yours and release others to find theirs. We deserve to be with people who want to be there. We deserve to build communities who truly see us, and that isn't possible when we're faking happy. We deserve to release the things, people, and places that no longer serve us.

I wanted romance, but I settled for palatability. I was palatable to my family, my friends, and even my partner. I wanted excitement, but I settled for comfortability. I wanted love, but I I settled for people who loved me. There is risk in the unknown, there is risk in letting go, and there is risk in goodbye. I am an only child, Virgo, Enneagram type 8, so I don't do risk. In the end, I had to let go of my relationships that were not serving me or my partners. And that's a good thing.

How many of us have found ourselves in situations that played out similarly? Not just with a romantic partner but with friends, family, bosses, jobs, and even places? How long past our expiration date have we stayed just to hold on with our fists balled tightly hoping for anything other than the inevitable outcomes.

Rejecting Harm

Some endings come from life cycles, and others come from harm. You do not have to keep anyone in your life, and you certainly do not need to keep people who cause you harm. It doesn't matter if they are your family, your partner, your neighbor, or your mentor. You deserve safety.

We are deserving of safety at all versions of our mess.
We are deserving of love at all versions of our mess.

We are taught to roll over from a young age. Always say sorry, be the bigger person, do more, spread yourself thinner, and accept that hurt that you feel. From a young age we are taught that our pain and our experiences do not matter if they make others uncomfortable. Too often that discomfort isn't discomfort at all but shame. People would often rather become defensive than to admit fault or to admit that they have caused harm.

Instead, we are expected to dance around their shame until their shame becomes our own.

I no longer allow people who cause intentional harm to share spaces with me; my peace is too valuable and so is yours. I have purged my social media, my contact list, and my real life friends list. Too many people exist in the outskirts of our lives not because they care about us but simply to remain updated on our lives or to maintain the status that staying in our life may bring them.

Rethinking Your Interactions

Many people want everyone to think they know you, but far fewer want to actually know you. It's time to spring clean your daily interactions. Ask yourself, do these interactions bring me joy or stress? Do these interactions make me feel excited, or am I filled with dread before having them? Does this person pour into my cup or do they only drain me?

The Internet has multiplied the amount of interactions we are capable of each day, and I am not only talking about your close friends. Whom you follow on social media matters, the trolls you argue with on Twitter matter, and the news you consume matters. They all impact your mental health, your well-being, and, quite frankly, your life. The Internet can seem as if it is not "real life," but the one thing I can promise you is that the energy you spend online is real, good or bad. The Internet just like a person can pour into you or it can drain you; you get to choose how you spend your time there.

How many times do you think you pick up your phone a day? Twelve? Two hundred? A thousand? How much time do you spend scrolling and staring into the lives of others and playing the comparison game? The Internet has many good uses, but that is not one of them. It may seem harmless, but comparing yourself to others will only further you from your authentic self. You do not need a perfectly curated life. Perfect doesn't exist; it is an online façade created by edited apps and mood lighting. The people you compare your life to online aren't perfect either; they are just not showing you their mess.

The Internet is such a wonderful tool, so why do so many of us use it in ways that end up being harmful for our mental health? It's simple: the quick dopamine hit. We're quick to shoot back an insult at a Twitter troll but not quick to mute them. We are quick to scroll through our high school nemesis' Instagram with a friend to find out if they got divorced, but not quick to empathize in how damaging that can be. We are quick to engage in the harmful behavior, yet rarely are we quick to engage in the healing behavior.

You don't have to keep arguing with those people from your hometown on Facebook about politics; just block them. You do not have to stay connected to the girl who bullied you in middle school to be the bigger person. You don't have to have Thanksgiving with the aunt who made racist comments last Christmas just to keep the peace.

Growth and Change Are Messy

You don't have to do anything that feels inauthentic to you. You just have to learn to not run from conflict and change. Even for those of us who swear we are adaptable, humans enjoy stability. Change can be one of the scariest things we ever do even though it is one of the only things that is guaranteed. Things change, people change, you change, and that is okay.

As you start to show up in your messy vulnerability, people will not just walk away, but they will run. Humans hate mess; we prefer to be able to compartmentalize, analyze, and explain away mess rather than experiencing it. The human experience is messy and to deny that is to deny our collective lived experiences. We don't grow from the mundane; we grow from the mess, we grow in it, and we grow through it.

Not everyone around you will understand that growth; let them lose you.

Becoming Rejection Proof

There isn't a way to put it eloquently, so I'll just say it: rejection sucks. I'd love to pretend that finding your voice doesn't come with that, but it comes with a lot of it. The world we have built, especially the corporate one, was not created equally or for all. It was always created for the "blueprint." The Jake from State Farm, red shirt and khaki pants, the rule follower, the well behaved, always ironed shirt, freshly buffed loafers employee.

Finding yourself and showing up in all of your magnificent glory will come with rejection. That rejection may look like missed opportunities, job interview rejections, dates that don't go as planned. Breathe. It is okay. That rejection, as much as it hurts in the moment, is simply redirection. The universe has a way of knowing who deserves your energy. So, what happens when you can't afford the rejection? Because let's be serious, in this economy, I recognize that we are not all afforded the luxury and privilege of choosing rejection.

Be selective with who and where you are willing to spend your energy on because when you are faking happy, faking corporate, or just simply faking it, you are spending energy, which is your most precious resource. If you have to fake it, that's okay, but make sure you have boundaries, support, and resources in place to help you cope, recover, and reground you in yourself. Spending time with our "alter egos" is exhausting, and you cannot pour from an empty cup.

9

The Power of Community

Your Support System Starts with You

There is a quiet myth we are told from a young age, a story that loops endlessly in the background of our lives: *You must be fully healed before you can deserve the things you want.*

You must be perfect to have the life you want. You must be, you must be, you must be, and you always push the goal post further.

You must be perfect—unaffected by trauma, with smooth edges, and no blemishes–and you must be unbroken to be worthy of love, joy, or success. We convince ourselves that we need to be the idealistic version of ourselves before we can step into a life of ease, vulnerability, and truth. We tell ourselves that the only truth worth telling is the pretty one.

But here's the truth: **You deserve all of those things, right now, today.**

Healing is not a finish line you must cross before you get to ask for help, support, or love. Healing has no finish line; it is a

115

forever journey. You are not a car or motorcycle that has a depreciating value; your value exists because you exist. Your value is inherent, you do not need to prove it. You do not need to be in the right stage of life to be worthy of the good stuff.

All of us deserves to live in our truth even when that truth is messy.

Stop waiting for the healed version of you to pop out from behind the door one day; healing is not that black and white. All versions of you will experience happiness, love, pain, heartbreak, and agony. The version in which you experience only the highs doesn't exist; it is a mirage. It is the thing that keeps us on the proverbial hamster wheel of life.

We are chasing versions of us that don't exist. Healing can look like several steps forward followed by a leap backward. There is no end date on healing, simply growth as you move forward. If you wait for the final version of yourself to find your truth, you will still be searching for it on your deathbed.

First, You Need to Accept Yourself

One thing about me: I've always kept my private life private. I've been intentional about what I share online, carefully curating pieces of my world to show and keeping the rest tucked away. But separating your private life from your public life isn't always seamless, and sometimes they can crash together.

I remember during one such moment, I had a moment of panic. I had started dating someone new, and I called my mentor Zach in a complete full-out panic. This person did not fit into my brand, my idea of a partner, or my bingo card; I was worried it would be "bad for the brand"—BFTB, as we joke about in my relationship. The world knew me for a few things, and this person didn't fit into the version of myself that I had curated for the world.

I have always been outspoken about being a queer Black woman, so how would the world feel if my relationship looked any different than that?

I have always been an open book when it came to talking about my life, my experiences, and my challenges. Dating a straight white guy monogamously? That was not part of my public persona. Especially after I had been in a very public queer relationship for some time. Nothing prepares you for the guilt you feel when you have to explain yourself to the world. However, you do not owe the world an explanation. You owe yourself acceptance.

I was suddenly facing a version of myself I hadn't anticipated, and I wasn't sure how it would be received. I was facing a version of myself that I did not recognize, one I was newly meeting. If I was having trouble acknowledging this version of me, how would the world react?

In that moment of panic, I questioned everything I've ever said about myself. Would all of the truths I'd shared be viewed differently because of this?

I realized I felt shame, not in my partner but because my truth had changed over time. I had curated the perfect life for the world around me, and that life was changing. The perfect version of me wasn't so perfect.

In a moment where I should have been letting love happen and letting happy happen, all I could think about was how people would feel about me.

Would people still see me as authentic? Would they still view me as strong if my life looked uncurated? But over the last few years, I had to acknowledge something: As strong as I am, I want a soft life, an honest life, a life full of love. I wanted a partner who brings out that softness and someone who makes me feel safe and cherished. And unexpectedly, I found that in someone I never saw coming.

Did that make my previous truths untrue? No. Did it make my experiences less valid? No. Did it make me less queer? Also no.

This isn't a story about my partner though he is a peach. This is a reminder that when we let the outside world dictate how we think we should exist, feel, or show up, we lose. When we hide parts of ourselves because of shame, we lose.

When we let the outside world determine whom we need to be, we miss out on relationships, love, friendship, and moments.

I had spent so much time curating my life, I forgot to live it. I forgot that life is meant to be lived, not hung like an art piece on a wall for people to create their own interpretations of. You will spend years trying to fit yourself into boxes that were never meant for you.

Your truth does not need to make sense to anyone but you.

When I finally had the courage to tell Zach my concerns, he laughed and said, "Your brand is authenticity. You're being authentic even in the messy parts of your life." And that's when it hit me: I didn't need to be perfect to be worthy of love or success. I didn't need to have everything figured out to be deserving of joy. I just needed to be me, and that was enough.

You just have to be you, and that is enough.

The Art of Asking for Help

You do not have to do this alone, at work or in life.

As a leader, it can be easy to feel you need to have everything figured out. You feel you're supposed to have all the answers, solve all of the problems, carry all of the weight without a complaint, and be the one people turn to when they are having issues. Unfortunately, as leaders we often feel asking for help is a scarlet letter, but it is one of the best tools you have in your toolbox.

The art of asking for help is often forgotten when we move into leadership roles because we are afraid to be seen as weak. But asking for help is rooted in vulnerability, self-awareness, and humility. It takes courage to admit that you do not have all the answers or that your plate is full and you are drowning. Asking for help is not a weakness; instead, it is self-preservation. When we ask for help, we open ourselves up to collaboration, support, and connection, and it shows your team that you do not expect them to ensure hardships alone.

Good leaders know when to ask for help. However, it isn't always easy to figure out how to go about it. Here are some ways you can begin letting others help you:

1. **Be clear.**
   - Instead of dancing around the topic at hand, be clear about what you need and why you need it.
2. **Tell it like it is.**
   - Acknowledge what you don't know, without shame.
   - Be candid about the challenges you are facing with the issue at hand.
3. **Trust your team.**
   - Empower your team members by acknowledging that you trust them and their skillsets.
   - Let go of the reins, and let other people take over; trust them.
4. **Support your team.**
   - Make asking for help a normal part of your team's routine!
   - Start Monday mornings with a meeting and ask, "What do you need help with this week" or "How can the team support you this week?"
5. **How am I doing?**
   - As a leader, there is always a power dynamic sitting in the room with you; ensure that you solicit feedback.

Give your team the space to give you feedback (good or bad).

6. Communicating collaboratively > delegating.

- Instead of demanding help or support, ask kindly and approach the work as a team effort rather than dictating roles to people.
- Instead of saying "Help me with this project," say "Can we figure this out together?" or "What are your thoughts on how we can approach this?"

7. Acknowledge your team!

- Show your team members appreciation (always) but especially when they step up to help accomplish a task

8. Find your squad.

- Surround yourself with people who are smarter than you, and that means at and outside of work. Ensure that your circle has people whom you can go to for guidance and questions.
- In return, make sure that when people come to you for guidance or questions, you are willing to lend them a helping hand.
- Support must be cyclical.

9. You are a mirror.

- Allow your team to see you asking for help to ensure that they know they are supported and empowered to do the same.

10. It's okay to not be okay.

- Leadership can be lonely and stressful, and sometimes we need more than our friends or a day off to manage. It is okay to need help from a therapist or counselor.

In my own leadership journey, I've learned to ask for help often, whether it be at work, from a mentor, or from my peers.

It is one of the most powerful lessons I have learned. As someone who grew up as an only child, asking for help did not come naturally to me; I always felt that I would be considered more capable if I always solved the problem before anyone noticed there was one. In doing that, all I did was signal to those around me that I was not open to help or support and I was willing to sacrifice my own well-being for work. By doing that, I taught my teams that they must never come to me with problems because that is what I modeled to them. Recognizing that is the first step in changing it.

Building Networks and Mentorships with Intention

What I have realized as an adult is making friends and finding mentors isn't as easy as the books make it out to be. Networking is awkward, reaching out cold feels transactional, and where are we supposed to meet people anyway?

An important part of your network is your mentor. Finding a mentor shouldn't be about finding the "best" person, it's about finding someone who sees you, who is open to challenging you and who doesn't view you as competition. It is easy to surround yourself with people who do not care if you win, or even worse, wish for your downfall, but finding people who are truly rooting for you is a gift.

Often when we think of mentors, we immediately start thinking of how we can access the smartest, richest, or most experienced person, but what if we thought about mentorship differently?

When looking for a mentor, look for someone whose leadership style speaks to you and who's mind inspires you. Whether in real life or online, don't be afraid to shoot your shot. One of my favorite mentors-turned-friend is someone whom I reached out to on LinkedIn and simply asked her if she would like to connect with me. Angela has since been one of my strongest supporters—and someone who became a very good friend. Over the years, I have come to her for help and advice, and vice versa, and all it took was a single InMail on Linkedin.

Our friendship is not a one-way street. I show up for her the way she shows up for me. I root for her the same way she roots for me. Mentorship, friendship, and relationships in general should not be transactional—growth does not come from transaction but intention.

So, how do you build a network of people ready to support you?

Building a strong, intentional network takes more than just showing up—it takes strategy, authenticity, and a willingness to nurture real relationships. Here's how you can do it:

1. **Whom do you want to meet?**

   Are you looking for mentors? Are you looking for well-known people in your industry? Are you looking to interact with people who are at a certain company or in a certain location?

2. **Be you.**

   This is not about impressing people or having the coolest résumé. Just be you; you are your super power, so lead with that. Don't forget to be honest with people about why you're interested in connecting.

3. **Offer support.**

   Do not slide into people's DMs with nothing but an ask. Offer support, and ask others how you can be of value to them.

4. **Research where the right people hang out.**

   Join industry meetups, attend conferences, and go to roundtables that are centered around your industry or the industry you are looking to enter. Find online forums/groups that pertain to your areas of interest.

5. **Social media is your friend.**

   Platforms like LinkedIn, X, Instagram, and TikTok are powerful tools for networking. During COVID, we learned the value of remote networking, and luckily it has remained a powerful source of connection. Don't just connect aimlessly with people—engage with their content, create your own, and get out of your comfort zone.

6. **Make a first move.**

   Don't be nervous. Reach out to people you admire, send that influencer a DM; take a risk. Don't wait for people to come to you; make the first move.

7. **Don't be a stranger.**

   All relationships require regular care. Stay in touch with people and check in on them, congratulate them on their wins, and offer support where you can. Don't wait until you need something to reach out to people. No one wants one-way relationships, even in networking.

8. **Curate your network.**

   Not every connection you make needs to become your best friend, but find people whom you enjoy spending time with, whose values align with yours, and who aren't afraid to challenge you and hold you accountable. More importantly, spend time making sure that the people you surround yourself with actually care about you and don't just want something from you.

   The right network isn't about having people who have the most followers or the most clout; it's about who is willing to build with you, help you, and support you when things get tough.

You don't have to be good enough; you just have to be human enough. Networking isn't about cheap professional small talk; it's about cultivating relationships, connections, and community. Your network doesn't have to consist of only people like you—I would challenge you to intentionally include people who challenge you, who are different than you, and who exist differently than you do.

It has to be more than collecting and throwing away business cards, LinkedIn connections, and cold emails. You can do all of that, and the people on the other side may never remember your name. True networking is about fostering connections. You must be willing to be vulnerable, consistent, and honest. You will need to be present, offer support, and check in with people and not just when you need something.

Intentionally build your network to reflect the kind of people you want to surround yourself with. In this day and age, your network can and will be more valuable than your résumé. Oftentimes, our fear of rejection keeps us from building a network and building community because we don't feel "good enough."

Asking for Help Is a Strength

Oftentimes, realizing you need help leaves you questioning your worth, your skillset. Understanding my own needs and not relating them to my own self-worth was a journey and not a comfortable one. I was accustomed to believing that I had to be able to be superwoman in all parts of my life, work, home, and otherwise. Realizing that I could ask for help and outsource things when I need to was a relief, but I felt a little guilty.

Today is the day to put down the guilt. You do not need to feel guilty for doing the things that make your life easier.

Realizing I didn't have to do everything alone was a relief, but it also felt unnatural. We are so taught to be independent that we don't realize that level of independence can often be a trauma response that stems from the feeling of not being able to depend on people from our past. There will be people who let you down, but so many people will surprise you with their willingness to support and show up for you.

Let your walls come down, and let people help you. When and if people let you down, it is not a reflection of you but of them, and quite frankly, there is no escaping that not everyone is for you, but the people who are will make letting your guard down worth it.

Asking for help isn't just a silly little suggestion; the data back it up. Research has shown that teams with leaders who ask for help have higher levels of engagement and trust. A Harvard Business Review study found that 67% of teams reported higher levels of trust in leaders who openly admitted that they didn't have all of the answers and asked for help. Why? Because asking for help humanizes you and shows you are adaptable, willing to learn, and willing to admit fault.

You don't have to have all of the answers, and you don't have to know everything; you just have to know how to be self-aware enough to recognize when you need to call in for back up. Our teams are meant to support us, and we should be hiring people who are smarter than us. It is okay to lean on them, and it is more than okay to acknowledge when they know more than you. Our world moves so fast with new information always popping up, and none of us can know everything.

When we ask our teams for help, we don't just help ourselves; we help them. Asking our teams for help empowers them to speak up, to contribute, to show their skills, and to collaborate. We do our teams a disservice when we lock our struggles and problems away instead of opening them up for collective problem-solving. The best thing we can do to create productive teams is to cultivate a culture of openness where everyone has the opportunity to share their problems, ideas, and visions. Humans thrive in community, and opening ourselves up to these conversations builds just that.

Your ability to show up imperfectly lets your team members know that you do not expect them to be perfect, and you will show up for them on their bad days as much as their good days. Growth comes from acknowledging our pain points, not from running from them, and that is a lesson worth sharing with your teams.

I have learned that when I show my teams that it is safe to make mistakes, it allows them to feel they can innovate more freely. Our possibilities are limitless when we do not have to be scared to fail. When we fail openly and gracefully, it lets everyone know that they can fail, too, because failure is indeed part of growth.

Learning to ask for help is not just a skill worth learning at work but also in your personal life. We need a little help sometimes, but it often feels easier to lock yourself with your heavy heart. Let people help you, whether its family, friends, or a partner, and do not feel as if you must navigate big feelings, big moments, and hard times alone. We need help sometimes, and we need community. Sometimes, you need someone to listen, and sometimes, you need a ride to the airport—don't be scared to lean on your community when you need them. The right people always show up.

You are not meant to carry everything by yourself, and the sooner you learn that, the better.

I have found that learning to ask for help at work has helped me learn how to do that in my personal life. It has been a great form of practice and has opened me up to not feeling as if in order to be considered a capable adult, I must be willing to make my life as hard as possible.

You must coach yourself constantly on asking for help, which means you have to unlearn the idea that you deserve a hard life or that you deserve the struggle and hardship. You don't. Struggle and hardship exist in all aspects of life: for everyone, even the best people. Although our struggles may differ from one another, everyone experiences hard things, and no one is "deserving" of them. They are simply part of life.

Life does not have to be a constant struggle. Find the loopholes that make your life easier; it is not cheating, I promise!

Therapists and Counselors Are Valuable Resources

Sometimes help from a team, our network, or family isn't enough. Leadership can be stressful, scary, and overwhelming. It is okay to not be okay, and it is necessary to be willing to admit that to yourself. Sometimes, we require help from someone who's job it is to help us sort through our mind.

And that is okay!

There is nothing wrong with therapy, counseling, and taking care of your mental health. The same way you visit the doctor when you have a cold, don't be ashamed to do the same thing for your brain. The world can be a scary place, and paired with the pressure of our jobs, it's easy to feel you've lost control, and the world is falling out from under you. Sometimes, you find yourself questioning everything from your career to your life choices to your own value.

You do not have to carry that alone, and sometimes, it is more beneficial to your well-being to talk to a therapist rather than your friends. Sometimes, it feels more natural to tell your friends, family, and partner because they love you, but a therapist is trained to help you sort the issues you are having.

Your friends and family can offer a listening ear, but they cannot offer an unbiased opinion because they love you. A therapist can offer you unbiased perspectives, strategies, and tools to help you work through your feelings and come out on the other side.

Therapy isn't a last resort; it is simply a tool available to you. There is no shame, no judgment, and no history with therapists. They are simply there to help you strategize and create a plan for yourself. Therapy is a safe space for you to explore all your feelings and experiences without worrying if they will think differently of you—they won't.

How You Treat People Matters

None of us has it all together, we are all new to this thing called life, and we are all winging it. Repeat after me: We are winging it. Every CEO, every executive, and every person you meet is winging it in some form or fashion. You're experiencing this life for the first time; give yourself from grace.

So, the next time you're feeling stuck or overwhelmed, remember that needing support is not a weakness. In fact, knowing what you need is a strength. You will not be remembered for the mistakes you made, but you will be remembered for how you treated people when you were stressed, upset, or overwhelmed.

We forget that under pressure we often experience emotions that don't reflect our true selves, and we may lash out, say hurtful things, or act in a manner that wouldn't be normal for us. Although stress is hard to deal with, as a leader you must be aware of how you treat people regardless of what you're going through.

You are responsible for how you treat people, and you are responsibile for how you treat yourself—so do yourself a favor and let people help you.

Care Is Mutual

It is important that regardless of where you are in your journey that you have people in your circle whom you can rely on, lean on, and go to for help. However, care is reciprocal. You cannot ask people to pour into you and return nothing to them. You must be willing to show up for your people in the way they show up for you.

Networks and community are all about connection. Community cannot be one sided. Creating a community that rallies around you works only when you also rally around community members. It can become easy to get caught up in "what you get out of it," but it's important to remember that you are also part of the community, not just a benefactor of it.

When we show up for others in the same way that they show up for us, that is where the magic happens, the special sauce if you will. It creates a space where everyone can feel seen, listened to, and cared for. There must be a balance between giving and receiving; that is what keeps communities strong and allows them to grow.

Care is mutual.

Sometimes, it feels like we don't know how to help, how to step in and offer it, or how to ask someone if they need it, but sometimes support is just listening, and sometimes support is just checking in.

- **Check in with your people**: Don't just reach out to people when you need them; reach out often and regularly.
- **Listen to understand**: Listen to people to truly understand them, not to respond or to debate them.
- **Say thank you**: When people are close to us, it seems like thank yous become less common. Don't forget to show gratitude.

- **Celebrate them**: Celebrate others the way they celebrate you.
- **Boundaries**: Set your own, but ensure to ask about and respect the boundaries of your community as well.
- **Consistently consistent**: Show up when you say you will, call when you say you will. *TLDR: Keep your word.*

The more we show up for others, the more they can and will show up for us. Not because they owe us or because it is a transactional relationship but because the more we show up for one another, the more we begin to show one another who we really are.

The more people get the opportunity to share themselves and share in return, the more trust we can have for each other and in our communities. That kind of reciprocity is what makes these spaces feel safe. When people do not feel they have to bear the weight of the world alone, the more likely they are to open up, blossom, and thrive; this is true for our workplaces, but it is also true for the people in all corners of our lives.

It cannot be about keep score or tallies of who owes whom what. It is about showing up when people need you and making sure the people around you feel supported in the same way you want to feel supported. And when we take turns showing up for one another, the group as a whole becomes more resilient, more compassionate, and stronger.

We are all stronger together than we are on our own.

At the end of the day, the best communities and support networks are the ones where people feel they belong and feel they can rely on those around them. When everyone is comfortable giving and receiving help, the better we become.

This is your reminder that we are all in this together, every single one of us. At some point, we need help, and none of us is meant to experience life alone. There is power in showing up for each other and creating space for healing and growth; this type of strength benefits not just our communities but the world around us.

To sum everything up, asking for help doesn't make you weak; it makes you human. However, you cannot only reach out to people when you need them; you must also be a person who others can rely on.

Community makes the world a better place; it's a reminder that we are not so alone on this big floating rock. We are surrounded by people who care, who love us and who want to see you win. Community humanizes the world for us and makes the dark corners seem a bit brighter.

The world can be a scary place, and we need support, whether it be for the small things, the big things, or just for a much needed laugh.

The balance of giving and receiving is how we build stronger futures, relationships, and deeper senses of community. All of us have something to offer, and we have something to ask for, and you are stronger for both of them.

Embrace both sides of this dynamic, and remember you are not alone; you just have to be brave enough to remember to reach out and touch the world around you.

10 | You Have Always Been the Place

"We often block our own blessings because we don't
feel inherently good enough or smart enough or pretty
enough or worthy enough....You're worthy because
you are born and because you are here.
Your being here, your being alive makes worthiness
your birthright. You alone are enough."

—Oprah Winfrey

What's Your Name?

How old were you when you realized you had never said your name out loud to yourself?

How old were you when you first introduced you to yourself? How old were you when your own name stopped sounding like a foreign language in your mouth? For so many of us, we have yet to properly introduce ourselves to the world and to each other. We spend so much time consumed by curating the right look, the right voice, and the right image for the world, instead of thinking about who we need to be for ourselves.

Sometimes, I still hear my own name and forget to turn around when it's being called. Sometimes, when I hear my name I am transported back to the person I thought I needed to be; I get flashbacks to when I was trying to fit into a box that was never made for me.

We don't speak often about the importance of our names, yet so many of us are asked to dilute them by turning a blind eye when they are mispronounced, coming up with "easier to say nicknames," or creating an "American-sounding name." Your name is yours; do not let others steal it from you. It is yours and no one else's. Your name is yours to have, to change, to do what you want with; it is not for others to decide. If your name doesn't feel right to *you*, change it. This is your story; hit them with a plot twist when you need to. You have the power to be whom you want and who you are. Please do not be bound by familial ideals, society, or the idea that you must just lie down and accept your fate.

Something that I have always struggled with is trying to live up to whom my parents wanted me to be when they gave me my name. I had to be a straight A student, had to be a top athlete, and had to go private school. I had to be "well rounded." They wanted someone who was bright and shiny, dentless. I lived a life that I believed they would approve of for a long time, but I wasn't happy. I was chasing the dreams of people who wanted the best for me but couldn't define what that meant. I had spent so much time trying to be the perfect daughter that I had lost sight of what life was supposed to feel like.

You must live for you. I feel incredibly privileged to have parents who "went with the flow" when I changed my look, my location, and my lifestyle. When I came home with blue hair, they were skeptical but moved on. When I came out as queer, no one batted an eye. When I came home with two partners, no one batted an eye. I recognize that not everyone will have that experience, and I am grateful for parents who actually just want me to be happy.

For those of you who are struggling with navigating familial dynamics and finding your power and your voice, please remember that life is not supposed to feel suffocating. You were not put here to live with the vice of society braced around your neck. Life is meant to be lived, fully, authentically, wholly. It may not always be exciting, but it should be light, like cotton candy at the fair, not like you are sinking in quick sand each step of the way.

Choosing Your Community

You do not get to choose the family you are born into, but you do get to choose who gets to stay family and who has the privilege of watching your journey. Yes, I said privilege. Access to you is a privilege, and you should treat it as such. Not everyone deserves access to you and the ever-evolving future versions of you. But that doesn't mean you have to go it alone.

Surround yourself with people who see you, and I mean truly see you, for who you are, who you've been, and who you will be. Surround yourself with people who are willing to meet you over and over. You can build the family you needed when you were a child and build a community for yourself that feels like safety. A grassroots community will always be one of the fundamental building blocks of radical change. We are stronger together.

One of the downsides of the age of social media is that it can feel easy to compare ourselves to people online. We may begin to feel envious of their accomplishments or frustrated that their journey is moving faster than our own. Instead of building community, we often seek to draw division because of our own insecurities. That's ego getting in the way. Do not let your ego win.

We are not each other's competition. We are sold a story that we must be cutthroat, prepared to cut anyone off at the knees who threatens our success. This is because they know how powerful we would be if we were partners rather than enemies. Our strength is not in our singular ability but in our collective power. Our egos sometimes shy away from community because of the "compare ourselves game." Check your ego at the door and build community.

Community building is not just about finding others with whom we can share our experiences but also about hearing the experiences of others to help us better understand ourselves. We cannot learn to check our biases or unpack our harmful ideas if we never hear how those same ideals have impacted others. Community is meant to make you feel seen, but it is also meant to make you uncomfortable, to challenge you, and to bring you closer to yourself.

The closer you come to yourself, the more power you will find in yourself. Society aims to lead us astray from our own bodies. It feels like so much of our lives are lived through out of body experiences rather than through ourselves.

You deserve to participate in life instead of watching it happen to you.

The Face in the Mirror

It took a long time for me to brave my own face in the mirror. I ran for decades from myself just to keep the world comfortable. I smudged my edges until I wasn't recognizable. I thought I could hate myself into a life that I loved. You cannot hate your way out of your problems. I hated my hair, my body, and my voice, and I thought if I just changed them, I could escape the feeling. You cannot escape the way you feel about yourself, you can only choose to understand it. Without understanding, you cannot find healing.

I would spend hours in the mirror critiquing my body, comparing it to the girls on Instagram, in Abercrombie ads, in my classes. I didn't look like any of them; therefore, I must be broken. As women, we are taught at young ages to hold our bodies to impossible standards, and I was no stranger to that feeling. Crash diet after crash diet. Fad workout after fad workout. My hips were still too wide, my legs too short, my face too round. My weight bounced back and forth, and even at my skinniest, I felt disdain for who I was. At a size 0, I still stood in the mirror defiantly, tears in my eyes, convinced I was not good enough. The issue was never my body; the issue was that I gave my body an impossible task: to look like someone who wasn't me. The issue is in believing that "good enough" is a standard set by an editor at a magazine who doesn't know you exist. Humans, bodies, and experiences are not monolithic. No one can define who you should be and what you should look like even when they tell you they can because they polled 200 people in New York City.

You are not a monolith; you are a garden.

You are worthy of your name and to look in the mirror without flinching. You must put down your preconceived notions about whom you are supposed to be, how your body is supposed to look, or what life you are supposed to curate. Look at yourself for who you actually are.

Stand in the mirror, and say your name over and over until it sounds like you are speaking to an old friend. Say your name until you say it with love in the background. You are your oldest friend and the longest relationship you will ever have. Make yourself a cup of tea and get comfortable learning yourself because how can anyone else know you if you don't take the time to know yourself?

You Are What Saves You

Our idea of who we are can be so skewed when it is shaped by everyone but us. Our families, our friends, our bosses, our jobs; they all have an idea of whom we are supposed to be. How are we supposed to make everyone happy? You can't, and the sooner we learn that, the closer to home we get.

Like a lot of people, I've experienced more than my fair share of trauma. I will never be the person to say that my trauma made me stronger; it didn't. My trauma left me completely unsure of how to move forward or if it was possible. I was riddled with anxiety, hyper independent, and unable to trust. But then I woke up and realized something that was truly life-changing.

Trauma isn't what saves us. You are what saves you. You are the knight in shining armor; you are the person you've been searching for in everyone else.

It has always been you. I have a tattoo on the back of my neck that reads, "You have always been the place." It is a quote from my favorite poet, Sarah Kay, from a poem called "The Type." Kay says that you can forgive yourself for your mistakes, and you are the place that you have always been looking for.

I got this tattoo when I left an abusive relationship as a reminder that I am always my own home, I am always my own comfort, I am always my own place.

It is easy to look for yourself in relationships, in jobs, in likes on the Internet. All of that feels easier than making peace with your past and yourself, but you will never find yourself in those places. You will find fragments of yourself, and you will find pieces, but you will not find the version you are looking for.

The trauma that I went through ended up bringing me closer to myself. It forced me to stop looking for myself in others and forced me to find myself in the mirror. It allowed me to invite myself in for tea; it allowed me to let my guard down with myself. It forced me to have to relearn everything I ever thought about who I was. Learning who you actually are can be both magical and terrifying. There is relief in letting your mask down, but there is the fear of knowing that not everyone is ready to know the real you. Are you even ready to know the real you?

How do you figure out who you are as an adult? Aren't you supposed to do that when you're a teenager?

There is no right time. Life is not linear, and neither is your journey.

Love Your Entire Self

If I could have learned any lesson sooner than I did in life, it would have been that I have to love me, all of me, not just the bits I'm proud of. It doesn't matter if others like me even if I don't like me, and not just the present me, but all phases.

You are not person you were five, 10, or 15 years ago. The past versions of you may not have always been the best version of you, and that's okay, but you must be willing to honor all versions of yourself.

You have to like those earlier versions of yourself, too; they're how you got here. There are versions of future you that may not be proud of who you are today; you have to love that version, too. I have learned that I am neither the best thing I've done or the worst, because I am not a thing. It's not easy to hold yourself accountable, but let love lead you.

Do not hold yourself accountable because you hate this version of yourself; hold yourself accountable because you love this version of you and want the best for yourself.

As humans, we will do good things, and we will do bad things forever.

To some people, you will be the worst person they know, and to others, you will be the best person the universe could provide them.

You can't love yourself only in pieces. You are the sum of your parts, not simply the parts we deem loveable. You are your best days, your worst days, the days that break you, and the days that build you.

You deserve to love yourself at all phases. All versions of your body. All versions of your mind. All versions of your heart. Forgive yourself for the person you were when you were just trying to survive because that person got you here: you survived.

Our magic is not just hidden in our lives but in our experiences and in our growth. We should radiate in our magic rather than run from it. We spend our lives covering our traumas, embarrassed and feeling weak. But our trauma doesn't define us even if it has changed us. We deserve to proudly call ourselves home; we deserve a sense of familiarity when we say our own names.

We deserve to look in the mirror and breathe a sigh of relief. Coming home to yourself should feel like a hug, not a punishment. Seeing the line around your smile, your eyes should fill your heart with the warmness of seeing an old friend.

I have never seen my friends' laugh lines and wished they had less, so why do I feel this way about myself?

We deserve to be our own best friend. We deserve to feel safe.

So, how do we begin to make friends with ourselves instead of enemies? The journey looks different for everyone, but I recommend you begin with being honest. All friendships must be built on honesty as the core foundation.

Ask yourself these questions:

- Would you allow a friend to talk to you the way you talk to yourself?
- Would you allow a partner to lie to you the way you lie to yourself?
- Would you let a family member hold you back the way you've held yourself back?

The journey back to yourself will be filled with uncomfortable moments, tears, and sometimes heartbreak. You are strong enough to meet yourself there. You have braved this life so far; you are strong enough to find a place to call your own. A place dug out in the inside of your chest, a place that you could call home.

I hope you choose yourself, I hope you choose to live, I hope you choose to experience life.

I hope you choose to be your place.

11

Joy Is an Act of Resistance

"You are your best thing."

—Toni Morrison

You Are Worthy of Joy

The world can be a scary place, and it often feels as if we are inundated with bad news, fear, and an overwhelming sense of dread. It often feels like when you put the news or social media down, you come back to 10× the fear you were experiencing before.

You log online, and it feels as if the joy is being ripped from your grasp, as if it is not something you are allowed to have. It feels like every moment has to be a fight for a better life, a better future, a better reality. And when you experience joy, you're tempted to hide it from the world because it feels misplaced, it feels inappropriate, and frankly, it feels like contraband.

But you do not have to carry the weight of the world's issues on your shoulders or become a martyr at the altar of the universe's injustices, even the injustices that you experience. Your joy is not a betrayal of how ugly reality can be; it is an act of defiance against the inhumanity that exists. Choosing to let happiness, laughter, and love in doesn't mean you're ignoring the pain of the world around you; it means you're refusing to let it eat you alive.

You were not put on this Earth to only experience struggle. You were not put on this Earth to only experience the worst it has to offer. You were put here to live, and to live means to experience the duality of pain and happiness, of heartbreak and love.

You do not need to sacrifice yourself to prove your humanity; your existence is proof enough.

There was a time when I felt ashamed of the joy that I experienced like I was undeserving of the small bits of light that had crept into my life. I thought joy wasn't something I was allowed to have because as a Black woman, you are conditioned to believe that life should be hard. It wasn't that I didn't want joy; it was that I didn't know how to embrace it without feeling guilty.

The world around us can feel so heavy, as if we are shouldering the burden of every bad thing we see on the news or on our feeds. It's all too loud, too much, too real—and how selfish of me would it be to sit back and enjoy my life?

How could I justify feeling happy in a world that was so broken?

How could I feel good about feeling good when that is never what the world intended for me?

I believed that joy was a luxury and that luxury was not reserved for people like me.

I thought luxury was a far-off tale reserved for rich, white men in Range Rovers. I thought joy had to be material things; I didn't realize that joy is so much more than that.

But what if I told you the best way to fight back was by seeking out joy?

> Joy is the first warm day after winter when the sun shines on your face.
> Joy is a perfectly made iced coffee (preferably pumpkin).
> Joy is holding hands for the first time.
> Joy is when your dog falls asleep on your feet.
> Joy is the silence of a library.

Joy is whatever you need it to be. Joy is deeply personal, and we experience it differently, but we deserve to experience it.

Find Your Joy

Joy is not something that you simply stumble upon one day; it is something you build, something you nourish, and something you grow. Many of us think joy just appears one day or that it is on the other side of our next big achievement or promotion, but joy isn't about your ability to be productive; it's about your ability to slow down and recognize what brings out the best in you. Sustainable joy is not linked to your career, your relationships, or your bank account; it's linked to you.

Joy is not something you earn; it is something that you have access to right now.

So, how do we go about finding what joy means to us?

- **What makes you happy?** So many of us are chasing dopamine instead of happy. We are chasing likeability, shiny new toys, and bragging rights. But what actually makes you feel alive? It's not the Instagram likes. What lights you up? What makes time stand still? What brings out the best version of yourself?

- **Put down your guilt.** You don't have to justify your best moments. Stop needing permission, and just experience the moments that make you happy.
- **Embrace small joy.** Joy isn't just in the big moments, but in the micro moments as well. Joy can be found in your ordinary routine or a song that makes you drop it low in the kitchen.
- **Take space to play.** May I recommend finding time to be silly? When was the last time you did something just because it was fun? Reach back into your childhood memories and think about the times where you were led by curiosity, adventure, and exploration. Harness those moments, and re-create them.
- **Choose joy, again and again and again.** Joy isn't effortless; it needs you to choose it. Remind yourself that even in the hardest seasons of life, joy can still exist. It doesn't take the pain or struggle away, but it gives you moments to hold onto and moments to look forward to.

Seeking out joy is about staying open to it and not shutting it out. Even when life feels hard, be open to trying joy out over and over again.

But let's be honest, the world has a way of making us feel like our authentic joy is something that must be earned. Whether it's personal issues, the weight of systemic issues, or just the general noise of the outside world, it can have you feeling you don't deserve joy.

When you hold a marginalized identity, you are conditioned to believe that your joy is tied to your ability to assimilate.

We are fed the lie that joy is conditional. Joy does not have to be earned; it does not have to be justified. Of course, the world is messy. Of course, some things need fixing and people who need healing, but that doesn't change that you deserve joy.

You do not have to put happy on hold.
You don't have to be fully healed to be happy.
You don't have to wait for the world to be better to be happy.
You don't have to have it all figured out to be happy.

You can be a work in progress and be someone who stops to experience and appreciate the moments they experience. You do not have to feel guilty for experiencing joy; you don't have to pretend you don't feel it.

We should all intentionally embrace more good in our lives.

The world will try to steal your joy, not because it doesn't believe you don't deserve it but because it realizes how powerful the act of joy can be. Joy is transformative. When each of us becomes grounded in our own happiness, when we choose to live authentically, we become the force that challenges the world around us.

They want you to believe that change is rooted in fear, but it is rooted in joy.

Joy allows us to challenge everything that is broken. When you embrace joy, you embrace your power. And that kind of power scares those who insist on societal expectations.

In a world where joy is the enemy of the good, joy is an act of resistance.

Start reminding yourself that your joy is not conditional; you deserve it just as you are. It's your turn; even when the world tells you that you must wait your turn, remind yourself that it's been your turn. You get to experience joy even in the mess, even in the despair, even in the face of adversity.

In a world intent on stealing every moment of joy from you, protecting your joy is the most revolutionary thing you can do.

Leading Without Losing Yourself

Joy and leadership don't often sound like they go hand and hand, but that's because we are taught to believe that work should suck. But it doesn't have to. Leadership will try to pull you in all different directions. You'll read books, listen to podcasts, and see on TV how you should show up and what parts of you to lock away. If you're not careful, leadership can turn into a perfectly executed exercise of self-erasure.

So many of us believe that leadership has to be heavy, it has to be a sacrifice, it has to suck the joy right from your life, but that is far from the truth. What if I told you leadership didn't have to feel that way? Would you believe me? What if instead of leading through burnout, fear, and power, we led instead through joy? Joy isn't something meant for us to simply seek after work, joy is a practice. The best leaders infuse joy into the way they lead, the way they collaborate, and the way they build.

Leading with joy isn't about leading through false positivity or ignoring the realities of the world around us; it is about leading from a place of fullness instead of depletion. It is about putting down the idea that good leaders must burn themselves out to be worthy of their roles, and it's about rejecting the idea that you must struggle to lead. Leadership is not about how much you are willing to or capable of enduring, but often it is about how much light you can bring.

It's about how deeply you inspire your team, and it is about how you can inspire others to step into their joy, into their power.

So, how do we actually lead with joy?

- **Be open about your why.** Share your purpose and your why with your teams. It allows them to feel connected to you as a leader but allows themselves to connect more deeply with their own purpose.
- **Take space for your *you*.** You cannot pour from an empty glass; to lead well, you must stay in touch with your own needs and prioritize health and self-care.
- **Make joy the rule, not the exception.** Joy is not a reward for suffering. Joy should be how we approach all situations on our teams, and we should be leading with humanity at the center. Create spaces where people are valued and seen at all times, not just when they check off a task on their to-do list. Make joy the foundation of your teams, not a nice-to-have.
- **Celebrate your people.** Leadership often focuses on the long game instead of the "now." Spend time intentionally celebrating the now and calling out the wins, no matter how small.
- **Set the tone.** Joy is contagious, but so is burning out. If you want to center joy on your team, you must embody it. As leaders, we are mirrors, and we must embody the behaviors we want to see on our teams. If we want our teams to experience joy, we must be intentional about experiencing joy ourselves.

Leading through joy is a radical act, especially in a society that aims to reward hustle culture and burnout. Unlearning the idea that work must be a struggle is a radical act and one that will impact your team well beyond their time with you.

Choosing joy, prioritizing it, modeling it, and leading through it aren't feel good tactics to put on your team value sheet; they must be the pillars of how your team functions.

You have the opportunity to redefine leadership, not just for yourself, but for everyone who interacts with you.

Leading through joy is not just about making people feel good but about doing good.

We are conditioned to believe that success must be synonymous with struggle, but what if instead of centering the "grind," we centered the needs of the humans whom we lead? Humans are not empowered by fear; they are empowered by the ability to openly seek joy. Joy and success should be able to coexist, and more importantly, they should be sustainable. We shouldn't have to grind ourselves down to nothing to feel worthy of success.

Not every day will be a good day, at work or at home, but joy isn't about just having good days. Leading through joy is about creating foundations that allow us to find hope on our worst days, to find peace in the chaos, and to find ways to build safety within our teams. Joy that is not sustainable is not joy; it's dopamine. Our teams deserve sustainable spaces where they can always show up, no matter the situation.

There will be many moments where this style of leadership feels counterintuitive to everything you know. There will be pressure to conform to more traditional ways of leading. However, true, impactful leadership isn't about how good you are at regurgitating the behaviors of the leaders you grew up with; instead, it is about how you can become the leader you always wanted. The best leaders don't blindly follow capitalistic expectations or antiquated methodologies—good leaders actually lead. And leadership isn't about how good you are at inspiring productivity; they inspire wholeness.

The Myth of Collective Growth

In the journey of seeking out joy, we often find that not everyone is meant to come with us. We often operate under the assumption that when we grow, everyone in our current reality comes with us. *Unfortunately, growth is not contagious, and not everyone chooses to evolve with us.*

In our ideal world, all of the people we love today will be the people we exist with for our whole lives. It's a beautiful dream to have, but unfortunately, it is only a dream. The reality is that growth is messy. Seeking joy, seeking authenticity, and seeking self aren't all rainbows and butterflies.

Like joy, growth is deeply personal. Growth is a lot of things, but it is certainly unpredictable, messy, and sometimes even painful. Not everyone in your sphere of influence will be ready to grow and evolve with you, and you have to see people for who they are, not who they may become in the future.

Your journey is not their journey. You cannot rush anyone's journey, including your own. As you grow into who you truly are, others may not know how to handle those changes, that reality, or the idea that you were never whom they believed you to be. Oftentimes, your growth may make others feel left out or threatened by how your joy takes up space. If your authentic joy makes others uncomfortable, that's not your fault.

You begin to feel more alive and experience life in new ways, but that authentic expression of yourself may shock the nervous systems of the people who were used to you having the curtains drawn. That new light may highlight their discomfort, their uncertainty, and their own struggles with joy.

People struggle to embrace what they cannot understand, and when people cannot understand your happiness, they are forced to confront how unhappy they may actually be.

Although it may not be your fault, it doesn't make it feel good or hurt less. It can leave you questioning whether you should return to your "old" self to keep the peace. You may find yourself wondering if you need to tone it down, but you will never have to tone it down for the people who are truly for you.

You begin to feel more alive and experience life in new ways, but that authentic expression of yourself may shock the nervous systems of the people who were used to you having the curtains drawn. That new light may highlight their discomfort, their uncertainty, and their own struggles with joy.

You cannot force people to grow simply because you have grown; you cannot make people do the work just because you're doing it. You cannot drag people along with you, and you cannot force people to be better, brighter versions of themselves if they are not ready.

How long did it take you to feel ready?

People's resistance and hesitation around your growth is not a reflection of you but a reflection of where they are within themselves. Not everyone will embrace your growth, but that doesn't make it any less real.

When you step into your truth, into your joy, and into your authentic self, it feels like you've opened the curtains in your home for the first time, and it takes a while for your eyes to adjust. But once your eyes adjust, you can see how alive things begin to look.

Does it hurt to realize that some people are only for a season and not for life? Of course. Especially when these are people whom you have always envisioned your future including, it makes their resistance feel like a personal attack but it's not.

This is where joy becomes fundamental because it's not just about how your joy makes you feel; it is about what your joy represents. Your joy is a love letter to yourself; it is a declaration that you are choosing yourself over and over again even in moments of discomfort.

Choosing authenticity is choosing joy, it's choosing peace, and it's choosing *you*.

How do we cope with their resistance, especially when it feels like rejection?

Ask yourself these questions:

- Is it my job to carry the weight of their resistance?
- Is it my responsibility to protect their feelings?
- Does their discomfort matter more than my happiness?

People who love you want to see you change for the better, and the same must be true for the people you love; you can want them to be better, but you cannot force them to be better.

The people in your life who truly love you will hold you accountable to this new version of you because love without accountability is just delusion.

The people who love you want to see you live in your life in full color.

But a goodbye for now does not mean a goodbye forever. You have no idea whom you inspire with your growth. Even if it initially made people uncomfortable, it may be exactly what they needed to take the first step in their own journey. Growth comes in it's own time, and one day those people may meet you on the journey.

Protect Your Peace

So, we've learned that growth is deeply personal, and sometimes, the people around you won't be able to keep up with you. You've felt the quiet tension of walking in your truth while others resist, you've sat with their discomfort, and you still have decided to choose you.

I'm proud of you.

But how do you protect this joy now? How do you move forward without continuously apologizing or reverting to the muted version of yourself? How do you hold on to that joy when the world is constantly trying to steal it from you?

The answer is in the art of saying no. Boundaries aren't always easy to set or even identify. It may feel uncomfortable, especially when dealing with those closest to us. However, protecting your joy requires taking ownership of what belongs to you, and your peace must be treated like the most important thing you own.

Only you can determine who has access to you. You get to decide how much of your peace, your energy, and your life you are willing to give people access to you. You can love people and still remain firm in your boundaries.

"This is who I am, and I won't shrink to make you comfortable."

Access to you is a privilege, and the only people who will be offended by your boundaries are those who benefited from you having none.

One of the hardest parts of stepping into your own authentic life is learning to stop apologizing for it. Beyoncè said it best, "I ain't sorry," and you shouldn't be either. Human nature is to want to please people, to make them feel comfortable, but the rawest truest version of yourself won't always do that.

Your joy doesn't require anyone's approval, and it is certainly not something you need to apologize for. You don't have to explain, justify, or define yourself for anyone why you have chosen to live authentically; the only person who needs to understand it fully is you.

Protecting your peace also means giving yourself permission to let go of the people, places, and things that no longer serve you. You have to learn to recognize when someone's discomfort is at odds with your growth.

But how can we do that in a productive way? Try some of these phrases:

- "This is what feels right for me."
- "I've worked hard to find this version of me, and I deserve to enjoy it."
- "I understand this may feel foreign to you, but this is where I am now."
- "I won't shrink to make others comfortable."
- "My identity is not a problem for you to solve."
- "I respect your feelings, but my life isn't up for debate."
- "I'm allowed to change."
- "I don't need permission to experience joy."
- "I can love myself and still love you; it is not a competition."
- "This is who I have dreamed of becoming, and I'm proud of that."

You do not need to apologize for changing or evolving, but it's important to be able to communicate your boundaries firmly to those around you. You do not have to explain or quantify your joy, but you cannot run away from the uncomfortable conversations that you need to have with those around you about that growth. Your growth is *not* an inconvenience, and your happiness should not be dimmed to avoid having the hard talks. Choosing you doesn't mean you have to reject everyone else, but it does mean you must stop running away from the interactions and conversations that you have been avoiding. Honoring your truth may come with a price, but that price cannot be you. The right people will walk with you in your new found alignment, they will bask in your light, and they will love you not despite who you are but because of who you are.

Speak with love, speak with care, but speak with certainty, with firmness. Don't apologize for stepping into your power; stand on business about yourself.

But here is the best part: When you stand tall in your decisions, your life, and your joy, people notice. You create a world where people feel safer to start to explore their joy, their self of self, and their journey. Your authenticity can be the spark that ignites someone's whole life; when you have the power to be a safe space for yourself, you open yourself to be a safe space for others—and that is what moves the world forward.

There will be days when it feels you are walking alone, because growth can be lonely. But even on the days you're unsure of how people around you will react, your authentic joy is worth protecting. You are not selfish for prioritizing your joy over someone's discomfort; you are simply human.

Give yourself permission to be human.

At the end of the day, protecting your joy is self-preservation. Joy is more than just a fleeting emotion; it's a revolutionary act, a life force. It's the thing that can keep us going when the world feels like it's too much, when people leave, and when life expects you to shrink. Without joy, you risk losing yourself to the world around you, to the expectations, to the judgments, and to the limitations that we previously believed about ourselves. Protecting your joy affirms who you truly are, safeguards your peace, and keeps you from falling victim to the external forces who want to keep you small.

The world will steal your joy if you let it, piece by piece, chunk by chunk; it will take to you like a sculptor with a stone, molding you into who it wants you to be rather than who you need to be.

Self-preservation isn't selfish; it is about ensuring you have the emotional, mental, and physical energy to keep going in this messy thing we call life. You deserve to thrive not just survive, but if you aren't protecting your joy, who will?

You are your best asset in the fight against the systems that want you to be anyone but exactly who you are.

Joy is your birthright.

12

It's Not You, It's Me

"I was told I wasn't good enough, but I just chose not to listen."

—Khalid

Community, Not Comfortability

You are enough, today, tomorrow, and yesterday—you have always been enough. All versions of you are worthy of respect, love, and community. However, if this is true for you, then it is true for all of us.

How do we begin to create spaces where we accept everyone for who they are and where they are at today, knowing that it may change? Too often, in corporate spaces, we expect people to be palatable, quiet, and a muted version of themselves. Even when we have done the work, these expectations must pop up.

So, how do we begin to actually unpack our biases, our preconceived notions, and the things that can make us harmful leaders? We talk a big game about authenticity and inclusion, but often it comes with an asterisk. That asterisk is to ensure that people stay "in line" and keep us comfortable. Good leadership is not about being comfortable.

Even when we have done the work, these thoughts and ideas creep into our leadership styles, without us even noticing. It takes a long time to unlearn years of conditioning, so give yourself some grace but learn to be better. We have learned that "professionalism" must dictate our work personas, but what is professionalism if not capitalism in a trench coat?

I recently spoke to a talent acquisition leader from a Fortune 500 company about how he leads his team when all of them are so different, and this is what he had to say:

> *"I'm not Black but work for a company where I'm expected to be palatable, nice, and quiet because that's the culture. I'm respectfully loud, educationally opinionated, and positively disruptive, which isn't the norm. But those are attributes I expect from my staff and appreciate when my Black team members voice strong opinions. I don't lead a team to follow me. I lead a team of thought leaders that bring various life experience, perspective, and expertise to every discussion without fear of repercussion from being who they are and expressing it. Their opinions are valid. Their identity is valid. They are valid."*

Good leaders recognize that being palatable, nice, and quiet aren't the keys to professionalism; they are the keys to power—good leaders don't seek power: instead, they seek community.

Let's Unpack Professionalism

We are fed the concept of professionalism from the time we start consuming media, from sitcoms to news to movies—we see the imagery of "professionalism" everywhere we look, and it often looks like men in suits and women in makeup, heels, and dresses—but do I really need to be in a dress to be good at my job? Absolutely not.

On the outside, we think professionalism is a parameter used to guarantee respect and kindness at work, but more often, it is used to be exclusionary and othering to anyone who doesn't fit the mold of who we deem to be "professionalism." Many of the expectations under professionalism are rooted in white supremacy, patriarchy, Eurocentric beauty standards, and classism.

A few years ago, I was speaking at a conference about culture and engagement when a woman approached me after the presentation. She began by telling me that she loved my portion and followed up with "Your company must be so inclusive to have you leading talent without a degree and being so *you* and *unpolished*." The word *unpolished* reverberated in my head for a few seconds before I realized what this woman was actually saying to me. She assumed because I didn't code how I speak or straighten my hair that I must be uneducated and she deemed that to be "unpolished."

I stopped her to inform her I actually did have a degree, and it was in the English language. I wish I could have recorded the shock on her face when she realized that she had just hurled an insult at me while thinking it was a compliment.

Oftentimes, professionalism isn't about how we treat people or how kind we are. It is about how we look, how we dress, how we speak, and even how we express and show our emotions. We are taught from young ages that all of those things must be dictated by what white, cisgender spaces have found to be acceptable.

Straighten your hair, soften your voice, wear the polo shirt—you do the things you believe you must to fit in.

Many times, dress codes prohibit natural or protective hair-styles, such as locs, braids, and Afros, and they are a direct result of Anti-Blackness. Black people have been denied jobs, passed over for promotions, and even fired for wearing the natural hair that grows out of their heads. They are told that to be "polished," they must be considered "neat," and professionalism has deemed natural hair as "unkempt." Obviously, this is not true; it simply doesn't fall in line with Eurocentric beauty standards. We are also expected to present with voices that are free of accents and dialects, which disproportionately impacts Black and brown people worldwide.

Additionally, people from Asian American cultures are often asked to choose Eurocentric-sounding names to be "easier to pronounce" to make them more approachable. We can learn to pronounce people's names, yet too often we choose not to.

People from all cultures and walks of life are expected to sacrifice their cultures in the name of professionalism. From Latinx workers being discouraged from speaking Spanish to Indigenous employees storytelling communication styles being undervalued, the expectation is widespread that we must be all fall in line and behave. It's also not just about how we look and sound but even what we believe: Muslim employees often face bias for needing to step away to honor religious rituals, while people in the LGBTQ+ community feel pressured to downplay their identities to keep the peace.

Professionalism should not be hinged on the ability to assimilate but in the ability to do your job: Who you are, how you look, whom you love, and what you believe in have no bearing on your ability to perform yet they are treated as if they do.

We use professionalism to erase cultural behaviors and norms to create spaces of "sameness," but sameness isn't safe, innovative, or even interesting. Many corporate spaces discourage emotional expressions as if emotions are not part of the human experience. Instead, they encourage stoicism, compliance, and detachment.

But whom does that serve? The leaders who insist on remaining comfortable. For so many of us, how we communicate is directly linked to our heritage, our cultures, and who we are. Many cultures communicate differently from their directness, body language, and even eye contact. However, for many, how they communicate is deemed as a threat to professionalism. Black women who are direct are labeled aggressive, gay men who present in a feminine manner may be considered "soft," and when we express feelings of frustration or sadness at work, we are told we are too emotional as if our emotions are a weakness.

The truth is professionalism was never meant to be for all of us. The exclusionary characteristics were built in by design, and the design works for those that it is intended to work for.

It is time that we build something different, something better, something that represents all of us. No more gatekeeping, no more letting our biases decide who gets a seat at the table. It has never been about capability but about comfortability, conformity, and control.

When you ask many companies, they believe that they aren't behaving in this way, and it's because so many of these behaviors are subconscious. These ideas have been so deeply ingrained into corporate spaces that we often don't recognize how we perpetuate harm.

You may be asking yourself, "Well, what policies uphold these standards?" Ask and I shall deliver.

Here are some examples (but definitely not all of the policies that uphold harmful standards):

Dress codes rooted in Eurocentric standards: Policies that ban natural Black hairstyles or ban colored hairs/nails.

Language and communication standards: Requiring employees to only speak English, policing accents, or discouraging dialects like AAVE or Spanglish, or asking employees to select "English"-sounding names.

Grooming and appearance policies: Enforcing rules about facial hair, makeup, tattoos, piercings, or religious attire that disproportionately impact marginalized communities.

Rigid work schedules and attendance policies: Penalizing employees for lateness without considering transportation inequities, disability needs, cultural needs, or care taking duties.

Eurocentric leadership and feedback styles: Valuing direct, assertive communication from some while assuming people from certain cultures are aggressive when they communicate similarly. Dismissing storytelling, collective decision-making, or other cultural leadership approaches and prioritizing Eurocentric norms.

Unpaid internships: Knowing all work should be paid, fairly. This sounds like a no-brainer, but internships are often still unpaid.

"Culture fit": Learning culture is just another way to exclude candidates and prioritize sameness in your hiring processes. (We'll come back to this.)

Gendered dress codes: Enforcing the gender binary by having gendered dress codes, such as requiring women to wear dresses or requiring men wear suits.

Policing emotional expression: Expecting employees to suppress emotions in ways that dismiss cultural norms around passion, expressiveness, or directness.

Performance evaluations: Understanding that too often performance reviews are given to reward those who "fall in line" with dominant cultures and penalize those who step out of those parameters. Additionally, evaluations that are given from subjective lenses rather than an objective one open the door for bias to creep in.

Culture Fit Is a Lie

Alright, let's talk about it: culture fit, the thorn in my proverbial side. Ironically, I used to subscribe to the concept until I realized in execution **it** doesn't work. The idea of hiring for "culture fit" sounds nice and it sounds welcoming, but in practice, it ends up being a locked door that you need a password to enter. It is exclusionary.

When organizations prioritize candidates who "fit" into their cultures, what they are really doing is hiring replicas of the people who already work there. Of course, that is the easy thing to do, but it doesn't move the needle forward, it doesn't create diverse cultures, and it certainly doesn't innovate. It may feel comfortable, but is comfortable the goal? No, absolutely not. The goal is to create environments where people can thrive, and people can't thrive if they spend their whole day just trying to fit in.

When we deny people because they are not a "culture fit," what we are really saying is, "Sorry, you're not enough like us; you don't feel familiar enough," and this will always work against diversity. What we're really saying is "You are too Black, too gay, too old, too fat," and the list goes on. People's ability to excel in a role has nothing to do with their ability to coddle the comfort of a leader, and they certainly aren't less capable because they come from a different background. These practices often impact LGBTQ+, Black and brown people, and others who don't fit the "dominant" mold at disproportionate rates.

What are we saying without saying anything at all? Success is a picture that is painted in white. Success has a predetermined mold, and that mentality will spoil your organization from the inside out.

Of course, it's an ethical problem, but it's also bad for business—and although I do not believe in needing to create a business case to treat people correctly, remember that diverse organizations build more diverse products, have more diverse customer bases, and have better retention rates.

The best teams are made up of people who share a similar goal but bring different lenses, backgrounds, and experiences to the table. Teams who are intentionally diverse are better at problem solving and outperform homogenous teams. In fact, according to a 2020 McKinsey report, companies in the top 25% ethnic and cultural diversity are 36% more likely to financially outperform those in the bottom quarter.

Additionally, according to according to a 2020 report by Deloitte, inclusive teams made better decisions two times faster with 60% better results than nondiverse teams.

Of course, no one wants to hire people who are harmful, mean, or unwilling to flex with the team, so what is the solution? Hiring for value add. As leaders, we should be constantly examining whose lens is missing at the table and intentionally think about how we can fill the experience gaps on our teams. Hiring for value add opens up opportunities for new perspectives and experiences and allows you to build a stronger, more trusting team.

At the end of the day, it cannot be about whom you want to be friends with or whom you want to spend a Saturday afternoon with. It should be about who can do the work, whose lens is missing at the table, and who can challenge you and your team in a productive way. When we rely on culture fit to staff our teams, we lose out on gifted humans.

Our goal should be to create teams that are dynamic and inclusive, and that evolves as time does and is adaptable to the everchanging state of the world. People should get the chance to let their true self shine, and to do that, we have to bury culture fit for good.

Dismantling the old guard of professionalism takes intentionality, which means we have to acknowledge where we or our organizations have upheld harmful standards or created unwelcoming environments. Owning the harm we cause can be hard and can feel shameful, but growth comes from being uncomfortable.

Our approach to writing policies shouldn't be rooted in "professionalism" but in safety, equity, and intentionality. Our policies shouldn't reflect how we think people should look or feel, but in creating environments that are equitable and safe for everyone who experiences them. So, how do we do that? Let me show you some examples:

- **Language matters.**
  - Avoid vague terms like *professional* or *appropriate*; these phrases are subjective, and open-ended terms leave room for bias to snake their way in.
  - Intentionally state that you welcome cultural, religious, and gender expressions are welcomed, and more importantly, they are protected.
  - Remove gendered language; instead of using he/she, husband/wife, mother/father, use language such as they/them, spouse, and parent(s).
- **Dress codes for function—not fashion.**
  - If a dress code is needed, it should be based on functionality and safety. For example, Occupational Safety and Health Administration (OSHA) has specific requirements, such as closed-toe shoes in warehouses/construction sites.
  - Create policies that talk about what is allowed, protected, and encouraged, such as natural Black hair styles like locs and braids.

- **Encourage communication.**
  - Ensure that in your communications policy, multiple ways of sharing information/feedback is encouraged, such as written, verbal, anonymous.
- **Be flexible because life is fluid.**
  - Remote and hybrid work gives access to employees who are disabled, caregivers, and those who do not have access to reliable transportation.
  - Reevaluate time-off policies to include floating or chosen holidays so employees can choose the days that are culturally or religiously relevant to them.
  - Give space when life happens to people, and it happens to all of us: a flat tire, a sick child, a morning that doesn't go right. We all have reasons to be behind some days, so give people grace.
- **Engage in bias-free hiring.**
  - Remove unnecessary requirements from your job descriptions. Ask yourself, does this role really require a degree, or are we being exclusionary?
  - Create structured interview processes with key takeaways and goals to help mitigate bias.
  - Ensure mentorship and leadership training programs are accessible to underrepresented employees.
- **Talk about pay equity.**
  - Ensure Human Resources (HR)/people teams are conducting regular salary audits.
  - Make salary bands public as it relates to career level and demographic.
- **Eliminate retaliation policies.**
  - Ensure your anti-discrimination policies have an even stronger nonretaliation policy.

- Create anonymous reporting channels for those who do not feel safe or comfortable reporting to their manager or HR.
- **Invest in education.**
  - People don't know what they don't know. If you expect your people and teams to unpack their biases and understand safety and equity, you must offer the education and tools to help them better understand our expectations.
- **Create access.**
  - It's more than Americans with Disabilities Act (ADA) compliance; it's about creating policies with disabilities in mind and not as an afterthought.
  - Accessibility does not begin at hiring; it begins in recruiting. Ensure all people who interact with your organization know that they can take advantage of accessibility tools.
- **Create a culture of accountability.**
  - Help your employees build community by creating space for ERG or cultural groups.
  - Hold people accountable when they cause harm even when they are top performers or have been at the company for a decade.
  - When building authentic and safe organizations, often-times, it means we have to say goodbye to people. Let people go who intentionally cause harm.

Equitable policies don't just remove barriers. They create workplaces where everyone can thrive. If your policies work for the most marginalized person, they will work for everyone else. Instead of creating a handbook that shields you from lawsuits, create policies that allow people to feel they belong and feel safe. The outcome is the same.

Hire Differently

I am a self-proclaimed hater—not because I hate anyone, just because I don't pretend to like everyone. It's okay, this is a safe place: you can admit you don't like everyone, too. However, likeability doesn't matter in hiring. You should hire people you don't like. It sounds wild to say out loud, right?

Well, stick with me.

It's human nature to gravitate toward people who are like us, communicate like us, or even look like us. Our brains are programmed to function that way. Humans are typically conflict averse, so we tend to lean toward people and communities who validate our perspectives and ideas. We find ourselves doing this at home, in our friend circles, in dating, and even at work.

As we are building our teams, it can often feel natural to hire people whom we "click" with. But if we only hire people whom we like, what we really end up doing is creating a team of people who never challenge us and who are our friends rather than our collaborators. When we prioritize likeability over experience, we end up creating a space where being different is discouraged.

You do not need to like everyone you hire, and you certainly don't have to like people to value them or respect their work. The best teams are built on healthy conflict and the ability to challenge one another's ideas and perspectives. Yes, conflict makes us uncomfortable, but being uncomfortable isn't a bad thing. Being uncomfortable is necessary, especially when growing teams.

When a colleague challenges our ideas, it's easy to feel defensive. Every challenge isn't an attack on your career, skillset, or character; sometimes, it is simply a different perspective. The ego is a powerful thing, and we often let our ego lead us. But our ego will lead us in the wrong direction every time.

Humans tend to take things personally, and that's normal because we're emotional beings. We often feel like critical feedback is a callout to our skills, competence, or our career. Feedback is good thing. You must remember that feedback, pushback, or even a challenge isn't about you; it should be about the work. If we internalize all feedback as insults, we will never feel truly comfortable hiring people who challenge us because it will feel like you've hired your high school bully even though you haven't.

When we take feedback as an attack, we miss out on the opportunity to get better, to be better. Whether related to work or leadership, we miss out on moments of growth. Accepting the feedback allows us to make better decisions, form new ideas, and can help us recognize any gaps we may have in leadership or otherwise.

Additionally, when we take feedback personally, it discourages our teams from providing us with more. Building a culture of feedback is pertinent to a functioning team. Feedback has to be normalized; otherwise, we risk never fully understanding our team or the dynamics within them.

Eventually, feedback will stop feeling like criticism when it becomes a normal part of how your team communicates.

High-performing teams aren't made up of just one kind of person; they are made up of multitudes. To build teams that are made up of all kinds of people, you must be intentional in your search, in your process, and ultimately, in your decision-making. Instead of asking your hiring team or yourself "Did we like this person," change your focus to "What perspectives does this person bring to the table that we don't already have?"

Seek out differences; it may feel uncomfortable but not only is it equitable, it's also a strategic decision to set your team up for success. If you only fill your teams with people who validate you, you're not leading—you're stroking your own ego.

You Are Not Alone

The world can be a lonely place, especially when it comes to feeling othered or ostracized. Experiencing bias and stereotypes can make us feel like we are alone, but I promise, you are not.

You are not alone in the things you experience. So many of us forget that the things we experience, feel, and wonder about are the same things that the people around us experience. So, why is it that we struggle to give space for others as leaders in those moments: Is it because you are not giving that space to yourself?

We are really quick to call out and recognize the stereotypes people think or feel about us, but what about the ones we harbor ourselves? That's a different story. We are hyper-aware of how other people make us feel, but not of how we make others feel—and that is where the real work begins.

It's easy to see how the world views us because we live it, and we feel the assumptions based on our identities, backgrounds, or our emotions. We feel those things, we navigate those things, and often we internalize those things.

What happens when we turn the mirror around on ourselves?

No matter how much we have been on the receiving end of bias, hurt, or assumptions, we have also been on the giving end even if that is hard to admit. Oftentimes, we are the ones making the assumptions and believing in the stereotypes without even realizing it. To be frank, it sucks to admit because the majority of us want to be kind, we want to be in community with others, and we want to be seen as nice.

However, if we want to begin creating spaces where people feel valued, we have to examine all the times where we made people feel the opposite. That means we have to question our previous hiring decisions or why we thought Chad was more capable than Brenda. It means asking ourselves how often we hired or promoted people because we liked them, not because we accurately examined who was best for the role.

I am not asking you to shame yourself but instead am asking you to examine where your biases have gotten the best of you. The more of our behaviors that we examine, the more self-aware we become. It allows us to see a little more of blind spots, and when we recognize where they are, we can actually do something about them.

If we choose to do nothing, then we cannot grow, and if nothing changes, nothing changes.

The Journey Is Just Beginning

As we move forward, dismantling how we have thought about work is not just necessary for ourselves but for our teams. We must intentionally reshape the narrative and how we think about "professionalism." We must no longer be reliant on the status quo and Eurocentric standards to dictate who is valuable at work.

We are not just advocating for authenticity and safety; we are building stronger, more inclusive, and more innovative organizations. We are building teams that are capable of navigating hard conversations and complex challenges. We are building the future of corporate spaces, and the future of corporate spaces should fundamentally suck less.

As leaders, it is our responsibility to create environments where people feel safe enough to take risks, give feedback, and can exist as exactly who they are without fear that it will be at the detriment of their career. An organization rooted in authenticity is one that inspires growth, trust, and the ability to see yourself reflected in your work.

Making work suck less may seem like a lofty goal, but if we spend 160+ hours somewhere a month, shouldn't it also be a place that feels reflective of ourselves and our teams? Although work can be frustrating, it should not become a place that is simply related to trauma and mistreatment. There is no reason that work should be the only thing we talk about in therapy or the reason we have a tummy ache on Sunday nights.

Making work suck less is practical. We should all aim to create organizations and teams that make people feel seen. Research consistently shows that people perform better when they feel safe in their environments. A study published in the *Journal of Applied Psychology* found that employees who feel safe in their workplaces (including psychological safety) have higher job retention and are more likely to feel a sense of loyalty to their organizations

As it turns out, you do attract more bees with honey, and the bees want to hang out for a bit.

If research shows that employees perform better when they are treated like humans with value instead of résumés with dollar signs, why do so many companies cling to the old way of doing things?

There are many reasons, but two of the most significant ones are:

1. People love power, period.

In many organizations, power dynamics are a badge of honor rather than something to unpack. Leadership roles, historically, have been about control, not about creating better organizations. That control may be about people, resources, money, or outcomes, but the end result is the same; leaders who lead through fear instead of humanity. Traditionally, humans have been treated as resources rather than people, deeming all people expendable and undeserving of humanity. Leaders may think that shifting away from these methods may shrink their authority, but leadership isn't about authority—it's about humanity.

Of course, maintaining the status quo feels easy. It will feed your ego, but it will not turn you into the leader that people fondly remember 20 years from now.

People in positions of power are often reluctant to give up power even when they have access to the data that show change would deliver better outcomes. It's easier to maintain a flawed system than to start fresh in an unfamiliar one. Unfortunately, the love for power comes at the expense of teams and people's well-being.

■ **So many organizations don't know they can do things differently.**
Another reason companies cling to the old guard is simply because they don't know there are other options out there. So many organizations have been operating under the same model for so long, and those leaders are leaving to start companies and just use the same model—so, it is recycled over and over again.

The old phrase "If it's not broke, don't fix it" often applies because the system works for who it is designed for, and if it works for you, you will assume there is nothing to fix. If this is always how business has been done and what was modeled for you, it is most likely what you will continue to do unless you do the work to better understand the needs of your teams.

Shifting cultures takes time, effort, and, more importantly, money, and some organizations are not interested in spending the time and resources to change and instead chalk themselves up to being "good enough."

Change is hard and weird, and to be honest, most of us don't enjoy it regardless of the quippy Instagram stories we reshare. We have to be willing to break out of the mindset that power holds the keys to the kingdom of success and recognize that if we invested as much time in others as we invested in our desire to climb the proverbial corporate ladder, we would all have work places that sucked less.

It's time to create organizations where all people have the space to shine and where all people are welcomed, valued, and empowered to be exactly who they are. We are redefining professionalism and breaking the rules set by people who never thought of us when they wrote them.

We deserve to bring whatever parts of us to work that we want, and that goes for our teams as well. We must move past the narrow idea that "fitting in" is better than standing out, which means we must create space for those who are different, who challenge us, and who make us uncomfortable.

Belonging, authenticity, and vulnerability must become the cornerstone of our leadership styles and our businesses. The goal isn't just about improving workplaces but creating better experiences for humans. Of course, there are business cases and data points that show us why we should do these things, but at the end of the day, we shouldn't need data to want to be kind, and we shouldn't need data points to want to be better humans, leaders, friends, and partners.

When we embrace holding ourselves accountable to create these spaces, we begin to be the change on our teams, in our organizations, and in the world. If we can make just even one person feel seen and valued, then we have changed the way the future may look.

If we can make one person feel safe, we can change the way people experience work.

You are the change.

Acknowledgments

First and foremost, to my parents—thank you for believing in me before I even believed in myself. You taught me to live in color, to take up space, and to always stand in my truth. I carry your love and lessons with me in everything I do.

To Charles Kim and Regina Brooks at Serendipity Literary Agency—thank you for championing this project from the very beginning. Your guidance and belief in me have been invaluable.

To Victoria Savanh and Kelly Talbot—thank you for reading my words more times than any human should ever have to. Your patience, insight, and care made sure these words landed exactly as they should.

And to my friends—Elizabeth Leiba, Kryss Shane, Aubrey Blanche, and so many others—thank you for catching me when the world was spinning too fast, for reminding me of my own power, and for standing beside me as I brought this book to life. You are my people.

Finally, to every version of me who paved the way to this moment: to the ones who stayed quiet, who shrunk, who survived in the shadows—I see you, I honor you, and I hope I am making you proud.

About the Author

Madison Butler is a storyteller, a space-maker, and a believer in the power of showing up. She has a heart for human connection and an eye for what makes people and organizations thrive. Madison's purpose is to help others shed the armor of societal expectations and lead with their truth.

She is known for creating spaces where tough conversations feel a little less scary and a lot more human. Madison weaves vulnerability, compassion, and a healthy dose of authenticity into everything she touches. She is an advocate for supporting mental health, destigmatizing trauma, and for being human at work and in life.

Madison is a trusted strategist to teams and leaders in all verticals. From technology to finance, Madison is committed to creating workspaces that make people feel like the best versions of themselves. Her approach is human-centric, transformative, and rooted in building organizations that people can trust.

Madison's voice has resonated far and wide, appearing in the *New York Times*, *Wall Street Journal*, *Cosmopolitan*, *Business Insider*, and more. At her core, she is committed to dismantling harmful systems and replacing them with a world that works for everyone. Her goal is to create spaces where everyone gets to live out loud.